The Private Secretary

The Private Secretary

Charles Hawtrey

MINT EDITIONS

The Private Secretary was first published in 1883.

This edition published by Mint Editions 2021.

ISBN 9781513280615 | E-ISBN 9781513285634

Published by Mint Editions®

MINT EDITIONS

minteditionbooks.com

Publishing Director: Jennifer Newens
Design & Production: Rachel Lopez Metzger
Project Manager: Micaela Clark
Typesetting: Westchester Publishing Services

Scenes

Act I "Found" – Douglas Cattermole's Chamber?
Act II "Full Cry" – Mr. Marsland's Country Seat.
Act III "Run To Earth" – Mr. Marsland's Country Seat.
Time in Representation, two hours and five minutes.

Act I

SCENE. DOUGLAS CATTERMOLE'S *apartments at* MRS. STEAD'S. *Comfortable but not luxurious. Doors, R. I E. and L. I E. Window practicable, R. C. fireplace, L. Sofa, R. c. Table with writing materials and books, L. C. Sideboard with liqueurs. Cigars, cards, boxing-gloves, etc., at back, L. c. Small table-lamp; at back, c., with papers, bills, etc.*

DOUGLAS *discovered, smoking cigar.*

DOUGLAS: (*L. of table, reading letter*) Of course, uncle's old fad again! it's enough to drive one mad. Any other man would be glad of a fellow living quietly and decently, but he's got the absurd idea into his head that I must sow my wild oats, and will do nothing for me until I've done so. (*rising and going to fireplace*) And I've no talent for knocking about. I've run up a few bills and I find that is all I can accomplish. And he's as obstinate as possible. When he finds I've been living quietly he is quite capable of going off and leaving me high and dry. When does he say he's coming? (*knock R.*) Come in! (*Returns to L. of table, picks up letter*)

Enter MRS. STEAD, *R.*

MRS. STEAD: Good morning, Mr. Cattermole. (*aside*) I'm determined to have it out with him this morning, (*aloud*) Good morning, sir.

DOUGLAS: (*looking up*) Ah, good morning, Mrs. Stead, I—

MRS. STEAD: (*coming to table*) If you please, sir, these papers have been left for you.

DOUGLAS: (*taking papers; opens one*) A bill! (*gives it back to her*) Another! (*gives it back to her*) And another, (*gives it back to her*)

MRS. STEAD: (*going up*) Shall I put them with the others, sir? I have put all the bills together on this little table. (*puts bills on table up c*)

DOUGLAS: (*L. of table*) You are a very careful Woman, I know, Mrs. Stead.

MRS. STEAD: (*coming down*) I hope I am, sir. But oh, dear, how is all this to end?

DOUGLAS: What?

MRS. STEAD: Why, all these bills are owing.

DOUGLAS: Yes; I only wish there were more of them.

MRS. STEAD: (*aside*) That's what he always says, (*aloud*) But sir, you used to be so exact, so very exact.

DOUGLAS: Well?

MRS. STEAD: And now you owe me four months lodging.

DOUGLAS: Yes. I wish I had never paid you at all.

MRS. STEAD: Thank you, sir, but I wasn't going to speak to you about myself, I have the utmost confidence in you.

DOUGLAS: Thank you so have I. (*turns up to fireplace*)

MRS. STEAD: But for the others, sir; how will all this end?

DOUGLAS: Oh, you wait and see.

MRS. STEAD: I think I can tell you beforehand. At present your creditors are all very civil, but by-and-bye they'll grow pressing then impudent till at last they'11 hunt you down like a pack of bloodhounds.

DOUGLAS: (*laughing*) Ha! ha! ha! That's funny!

MRS. STEAD: (*crying*) And you can laugh at that sir? I can't bear to think of it.

DOUGLAS: (*comes down c. on* MRS. STEAD's *left*) Oh stop that crying, my good woman, and listen to me. It's a very funny affair altogether.

MRS. STEAD: Funny, sir!

DOUGLAS: Yes you must know that I have an uncle.

MRS. STEAD: Yes, sir.

(*Knock heard at outer door R.*)

DOUGLAS: Who is very

MRS. STEAD: (*interrupting*) Stop a minute, sir, there's a knock at the outer door. Do step into the next room for a minute.

DOUGLAS: My good woman, I don't want to step into the next room.

MRS. STEAD: But do, sir, just to oblige me.

DOUGLAS: But why should I?

MRS. STEAD: Oh, do, sir, I'm sure it's one of the creditors.

DOUGLAS: (*going towards door L.*) But I am not afraid of my creditors.

MRS. STEAD: (*ushers off* DOUGLAS *L I E. Shuts door and returns to L. c.*) But I am, sir, I am.

DOUGLAS: But you won't have to pay them. Oh, very well. (*Exit L., knock R.*)

MRS. STEAD: Come in.

(*Enter* GIBSON; *door R. I E. exaggerated attire, large stick with much gesticulation, at times very affected.*)

GIBSON: Ah I Good morning, Mrs. Stead.

MRS. STEAD: Good morning, sir.

GIBSON: (*coming down R. c.*) Is Mr. Cattermole at home?

MRS. STEAD: (*hesitatingly*) I—I really don't know, sir.

GIBSON: The servant said he hadn't gone out yet.

MRS. STEAD: Perhaps it is that he hasn't been home all night, sir.

GIBSON: Very clever, but it won't do for me. (*sniffing, crossing L.*) Do you smoke?

MRS. STEAD: Smoke, sir! me, sir! no, sir!

GIBSON: Well, I can smell smoke.

MRS. STEAD: Perhaps it's the chimney, sir.

GIBSON: Well, then, the chimney smokes devilish good cigars, (*going up L. and seating himself in arm chair by fire*) Very clever, but I'm too old a bird to be caught with chaff like that.

MRS. STEAD: (*a little up stage R. c.*) Well, sir, I see it's no use trying to deceive you.

GIBSON: Not a bit.

MRS. STEAD: So I may as well tell you the truth at once. The fact is, sir, Mr. Cattermole came home late last night.

GIBSON: Oh, what a life these young fellows do lead to be sure. Heigho! (*sighing*)

MRS. STEAD: And why should you sigh like that, sir?

GIBSON: Because I can't live like them myself.

MRS. STEAD: You can if you like, sir.

GIBSON: No, I can't! Don't you know, my good woman, that I'm only a tailor?

MRS. STEAD: A tailor? (*aside*) It's Mr. Gibson!

GIBSON: That's just it! You see, if I were a common tailor, I could live in a common way. But that's just what I'm not. I hate and detest vulgarity, and have a longing for higher spheres. You know, as the poet says so prettily, I long to soar to soar well, not exactly into ethereal blue but on to the upper crust of society.

MRS. STEAD: Soar on to the upper crust! Good gracious! Are you in your right senses, Mr. Gibson? (*goes down R. c.*)

GIBSON: (*rising, coming down, L.*) Why, of course I am, my good woman. But prejudice, vile prejudice, Mrs. Stead. Now, I assure you, I very rarely flatter myself, but I. feel that there's all the makings of a first class gentlemanly article about me. Don't you think so, eh? Don't you like this style, eh? It's good, isn't it? I say, you don't mean to say you don't think I don't look like a gentleman, do you?

MRS. STEAD: Very elegant, indeed, sir but, then, with your figure

GIBSON: What do you know about my figure? You let my figure alone. My figure's not good. No, I don't want to flatter myself it's very far from elegant; in fact, it's wretched.

MRS. STEAD: Oh, no, sir; I'm sure you have a very excellent figure.

GIBSON: Well, you'll allow me to know something about my own figure! (*surveying himself*) This is not figure, my good woman it's cut! the embellishment of art high art! I am a believer in high art. And I'm a believer in the higher classes. I wish I could soar among them.

MRS. STEAD: I think you do believe in the higher classes, sir.

GIBSON: Yes, I only feel at home in the company of gentlemen; but, as I said before, prejudice, vile prejudice! Ah, if they'd only give me a chance, I'd show them what a part I could play among the exclusive aristocracy the upper ten thousand. I don't wish to flatter myself, but I think I should astonish the world, (*crosses to R.*)

MRS. STEAD: I think you ought to be satisfied, sir, with your present position.

GIBSON: (*with eye-glass*) I wish this glass would stick in.

MRS. STEAD: (*L. c.*) You have an excellent business.

GIBSON: What business have you to talk about my business? I hate my business.

MRS. STEAD: And you make plenty of money.

GIBSON: Money I Yes, I've plenty of money. But money can't buy happiness, can it, Mrs. Stead?

MRS. STEAD: No. indeed, sir, it cannot.

GIBSON: No, and money can't make a gentleman.

MRS. STEAD: All very true, sir.

GIBSON: And I flatter myself I can be a gentleman without the money, (*going up to door R.*) Well, good morning, Mrs. Stead, I shall call again and see Mr. Cattermole. (MRS. STEAD *turning makes gesture of distress*) Ah, by-the-bye now you seem to be a sensible woman, and know an elegant article when you see one. Now, I shouldn't be very much offended if you were to tell people that you thought I really was a gentleman.

MRS. STEAD: I will, sir I I'll tell them that you want to soar.

GIBSON: Yes, that's my sore point! Bon soir! (*Exit R.*)

(*At* GIBSON'S *exit t* MRS. STEAD *goes to door L., opens it to call* DOUGLAS, *then turns to R. c.*)

Mrs. Stead: (*laughing*) If he wants to soar, he had better go up in a balloon, (*calling L.*) Mr. Cattermole! You may come out now.

(*Enter* Douglas, *L., he goes L. of table.*)

    That was Mr. Gibson, sir; but I've got rid of him. And now, sir, will you go on?

Douglas: What?

Mrs. Stead: That wonderful story.

Douglas: Oh, that's soon done! You must know that I've an uncle

Mrs. Stead: Yes, sir; that's where we left off.

Douglas: Who is very rich.

(*Enter Harry quickly, R. I E.*)

Harry: (*coming down to table, and shaking hands with* Douglas) Good morning, old fellow, lucky you're here.

Douglas: Good morning!

Mrs. Stead: (*to* Douglas) Won't you continue the—

Douglas: By-and-bye, my good woman. (*turns up, L.*)

Mrs. Stead: (*aside*) Oh, how provoking, (*cross to door, R.*) How will it all end? (*Exit, R.*)

Harry: (*sitting R. of table*) Douglas, I want you to do me a great service.

Douglas: (*at fireplace*) If I can I shall be very glad.

Harry: You remember that some months ago I wanted three hundred pounds, and you gave me your signature?

Douglas: Oh, yes, I remember.

(Douglas *gets cigarette from box on sideboard, lights it c. then drops down to L. of table*)

Harry: That bill fell due three or four days ago.

Douglas: I know it did. The fellow came to me I told him I couldn't pay.

Harry: Well, of course not, and Jenkins won't wait. I had notice from him this morning that unless the money was paid before night he would have me served with a writ.

Douglas: Well, let him serve it, that won't hurt you. (*comes to chair L. of table*)

Harry: No; but look here, old chap, I have an invitation from my Uncle Marsland. You know he's the master of the Featherstone Hounds, and tomorrow is the first meet of the season. I have also a charming note from my cousin, begging me to be sure to come. Now, my chances in that quarter would be quite gone if I were not to turn up.

DOUGLAS: Then turn up, there's nothing to prevent you.

HARRY: But, my dear old chap, the fellow would be sure to find me out, and serve, his confounded writ on me down there. My uncle has the most righteous horror of a bill; and as to a writ, why he'd kick me out of the house.

DOUGLAS: Well, what do you want me to do?

HARRY: Write to Jenkins and tell him you'll be responsible for the whole thing.

DOUGLAS: But, my dear fellow, my signature makes me responsible. Depend upon it he'll get out two writs while he's about it. I'm in just as great a hole as you are.

HARRY: But then, your uncle would help you, wouldn't he?

DOUGLAS: Not a bit of it! Won't give me a penny till I've sown my wild oats, as he calls it.

HARRY: Then the sooner you start off to sow those wild oats the better.

DOUGLAS: But I've no inclination for that sort of thing. Now, if it was your uncle—

HARRY: (*interrupting*) Stop a moment! I have it! My uncle has engaged a new private secretary, whom he has never seen, and who was to have gone down with me to-day. I've got him with me here. Now we'll leave him here and you shall go down in his place.

DOUGLAS: Will that be sowing wild oats?

HARRY: Well, it's a beginning, and may lead to the wildest of wild oats, (*rising*) Here, between these four walls, you never will have much of a chance but there, who knows you may fall in love, and when a man's in love he's sure to begin to play the fool, and everything else will come of itself. (*goes up to door, R.*)

DOUGLAS: (*rising and going up, remonstrating*) But, my dear fellow

HARRY: (*interrupting*) Not a word! (*opens door; tails*) Mr. Spalding!

SPALDING: (*without*) Yes.

HARRY: Will you be good enough to step this way? (*closes door; goes to* DOUGLAS) This is the most extraordinary fellow you ever saw. (*Knock R.*)

DOUGLAS: Come in!

SPALDING puts his head in shyly, at door R.

SPALDING: I beg your pardon. Am I right?

HARRY: Oh yes. (*introducing*) My friend, Douglas Cattermole Mr. Spalding, my uncle's private secretary.

DOUGLAS: How do you do?

SPALDINGc How do you do? (*slight pause,* DOUGLAS *and* HARRY *are both up stage, c., chatting and laughing*) I hope I'm not in the way. (*going*)

DOUGLAS: Won't you come in?

SPALDING: Thanks. (*Enters. A very shy, awkward young man, dressed like a parson. Umbrella in one hand, goloshes over his boots.* DOUGLAS *and* HARRY *stand apart, laughing and talking, not noticing* SPALDING, *who is standing looking about him as if waiting to be asked to take a seat.*)

DOUGLAS: (*suddenly seeing him*) Oh, I beg your pardon. Won't you sit down?

SPALDING: Thanks! (*Seats himself on sofa; umbrella between legs; puts hat on umbrella; picture.*)

DOUGLAS: (*returns to sideboard, offers* HARRY *cigarttte, they remain talking till* SPALDING *speaks, then* DOUGLAS *goes to L. of table*) Have a brandy and soda?

SPALDING: No, thanks, (*points to Blue Ribbon*)

HARRY: (*going to him*) Allow me to take your Umbrella.

SPALDING: No, thanks. I might forget it. I would rather keep it, if you don't mind.

HARRY: Not in the least!

(*Smacks him on shoulder, and returns to* DOUGLAS, SPALDING *places his hat and umbrella by his side, takes off goloshes, carefully puts them under sofa, and takes off gloves.* DOUGLAS *and* HARRY *laughing aside.* SPALDING *smooths hair and dabs nose with handkerchief.*)

SPALDING: Would you kindly tell me by what train we start? as all my goods and chattels are still at the hotel.

HARRY: You seem to be in a great hurry. Don't you like London? (*takes chair R. of table and sits by* SPALDING; DOUGLAS *sits on table*)

SPALDING: Oh no, I don't like London! D'you know, (*points finger at* HARRY, *who starts slightly*) I'm so used to my quiet little study at home that my head gets quite bewildered with all this noise. Everywhere I see written up "Beware of Pickpockets." One is kept busy guarding one's pockets.

DOUGLAS: Oh, come, it's not so bad as that.

SPALDING: Oh yes, it is. D'you know, (*points finger,* HARRY *jumps*) yesterday I wanted some luncheon so I went to the British Museum to buy a bath bun; and there I met a gentleman who most politely told me they were just closing. He evidently saw that I was a stranger I don't know why and asked me to lunch with him. At first I refused, but he was so pressing that at last I consented, and it ended in our having a very good meal. D'you know, (*points finger,* HARRY *moves chair away*) that when he wanted to pay he found that his purse had been stolen.

HARRY & DOUGLAS: (*Look at each other and laugh, together*) *Oh, indeed!*

SPALDING: But, luckily, I had mine with me, so qould pay for him.

HARRY & DOUGLAS: (*together*) Oh, that was very lucky! How fortunate!

SPALDING: But that's not all.

HARRY: No?

SPALDING: No. To-day I met a young lady in an omnibus.

HARRY: Who had also lost her purse.

SPALDING: Oh, no. She had lost her aunt. She was so nice! She told me that her papa was a clergyman, and asked me to protect her. She was very nice! D'you know, we searched for that aunt the whole morning.

HARRY: Of course, without result?

SPALDING: Well, it resulted in a very grave expense. If this continues I shall spend all my money. Would you kindly tell me by what train we start?

HARRY: My good fellow (*slaps him on knee, rises and puts back chair*), I have just heard from my uncle. He wishes you to remain here.

SPALDING: Here in London? How nice! (*handkerchief business*)

HARRY: You will have no expenses whatever. My friend Cattermole, is going with me to-day and leaves his rooms at your disposal.

SPALDING: You mean that I (*rises*)

HARRY: I mean that you may consider yourself lucky, so without any more fuss, my dear Spalding (*slaps him on shoulder*)

SPALDING: How nice!

HARRY: You stay here! (SPALDING *sits, puts on one golosh*) You will fetch your things from the hotel, Your landlady is a charming woman, who has neither lost her purse nor her aunt. You will be well cared for and can live at your ease, so look sharp.

SPALDING: How very kind of you to let me have your rooms. (*takes hat*)

HARRY: (*with* DOUGLAS *leading him to door R.*) Oh, for goodness sake, no pretty speeches, if you want to see us again.

(HARRY *holding door open.* DOUGLAS *L. c.*)

SPALDING: (*turning c.*) Oh, you'll pardon me, but I've left my umbrella, (*going to sofa taking umbrella, returning to door*) I'll take it with me,

CHARLES HAWTREY

if you don't mind. I always notice that if one leaves one's umbrella it is always sure to rain. (*turning at door*) Oh, I have left my golosh I (*returning to sofa and fetching golosh*) D'you know, (*points golosh at* DOUGLAS's *face who starts back*) I suffer so much with chronic influenza that I am obliged to wear these, (*tries to put it on his foot*) With your permission, I will put it on. (*Business* SPALDING *hopping on one foot trying to pull on golosh,* HARRY *says "Allow me to help you!"*) No. I'll take it with me, if you don't mind.

(*Exit* SPALDING *R.*)

(HARRY *shuts door and stands with his back against it, laughing.* DOUGLAS *falls into arm-chair by fire.*)

HARRY: Got a brandy and soda, old fellow?

DOUGLAS: Yes, you'll find one there, (*pointing to sideboard*) What time does this train start?

HARRY: 1.15 from King's Cross.

DOUGLAS: (*looking at watch*) Then we've just got an hour to spare. What shall we do? (*picks up newspaper*)

HARRY: Oh, we can't go out. Here are cards. let's have a game at ecarte.

(N. B. *Cards to be "made" with twos to sevens at bottom of pack to throw out easily as for ecarte. Deal and play as for ecarte.*)

DOUGLAS: My dear boy, we can't play cards at this time of the morning.

HARRY: Oh, nonsense! Imagine you've been sitting up all night, and then you'll think nothing of it. Shall I begin?

(*They come down to table, and sit and play.* DOUGLAS, *L.,* HARRY, *R. Knock at door, R.*)

DOUGLAS: Come in!

(*Enter* GIBSON, *R.*)

GIBSON: Ah, good morning, gentlemen! (*places hat and stick on small table at back*) How glad I am to find you at home at last.

DOUGLAS: Good morning, Gibson. What can I do for you?

GIBSON: Very little, sir. I merely called to inquire after your health, (*comes down to back of table*)

DOUGLAS: Thanks, Gibson; I'm quite well.

GIBSON: I'm very glad to hear that, sir, I'm sure. Some time ago I took the liberty of presenting my little bill. It's been mislaid, perhaps, eh?

DOUGLAS: Oh, no. I think not, Gibson. You'll probably find it over there (GIBSON *goes up to c. table*) among the rest.

GIBSON: (*taking up handful of bills*) Oh! I see it's not lonely.

DOUGLAS: Oh, I never forget a thing of that sort, But at present it's rather inconvenient for me to pay.

GIBSON: (*aside*) I thought as much.

DOUGLAS: Heavy losses at the Shark Club.

GIBSON: (*eagerly coming down*) The Shark Club, did you say, sir? Do you know, sir, I've heard a good deal about the Shark Club lately. I should very much like to go there myself. You couldn't manage to take me there with you some night? (*back of table*)

DOUGLAS: My dear Mr. Gibson, a club is a private house one can introduce one's friends but scarcely—

GIBSON: Oh, yes, I know. You needn't say another word, (*going R.*) Because I'm only a tailor.

DOUGLAS: But I shall be passing your door in a few days.

GIBSON: Passing my door?

DOUGLAS: Yes.

GIBSON: I'd much rather you came in.

DOUGLAS: Merely a manner of speaking, you know,

GIBSON: (*aside*) That's his manner of paying, too.

DOUGLAS: Won't you have a cigarette or a cigar?

GIBSON: Thanks! (*crosses eagerly to bottom of table and holds out hand.*)

DOUGLAS: "Oh, you'll find one over there. (*points to sideboard*)

GIBSON says "Oh!" (*goes up to sideboard and gets cigarette*)

DOUGLAS: Brandy and soda?

GIBSON: No, thanks! That's not one of my weaknesses. In fact, I've a poor head for drink at any time, but I can smoke (*takes cigarette; lighting it; aside*) Evidently wants me to make myself at home. Well, I'll show him I can be as much at my ease as he can. Lord! what a jolly life these young fellows do lead to be sure, (*coming down to table*) If I could only get in among their set. . . Ah! what are you playing?

HARRY: Ecarte.

GIBSON: Ecarte'! I'm a don at Ecarte. Jolly good game, (*looks over* HARRY's *hand*)

HARRY: (*to* DOUGLAS) I say, old fellow, I want cards.

GIBSON: No, you don't. (DOUGLAS *offers cards*)

HARRY: Eh?

GIBSON: Don't you propose you play.

HARRY: I wish you'd be quiet.

GIBSON: You don't want cards with a hand like that, surely to goodness.

HARRY: What do you mean?

GIBSON: Why, look here! You've got the king and the knave; the third point must be yours.

HARRY: (*rising and throwing down cards*) Oh, I say, this is too bad! You're exposing my cards! What the devil do you mean?

GIBSON: Why, you can't play the game. Here. I'll bet you a sovereign I win with a hand like that. (*puts hand in pocket*) Oh, no. I beg your pardon, I can't bet you a sovereign (*going, R.*) because I don't happen to have less than a fiver. (DOUGLAS *rises and gets c. at table*)

HARRY: At any rate, you don't know how to behave. It's very evident you're not a gentleman.

GIBSON: (*turning and coming up to him*) Here, don't you insult me! Don't you know that's my weak point?

HARRY: (*moving threateningly towards him*) Yes, I should say your weakest.

DOUGLAS: (*coming between them*) Now, shut up Harry! Gibson, you'd better clear out.

GIBSON: But he said—

DOUGLAS: (*interrupting*) I don't care what he said.

GIBSON: Oh, you, too, eh? You're a precious couple, you are! Why don't you pay your debts? I'm as much of a gentleman as you are. (*taking hat and stick from table,* HARRY *and* DOUGLAS *following him up, talking loudly*) This is the first time in my life I've been treated like this, but you shall suffer for it.

(*This to be worked up,* HARRY *and* DOUGLAS *saying, "Clear out!" "Can't you see you are not wanted," etc., etc. All talking at once.* HARRY *to keep over L.* DOUGLAS *and* GIBSON *R. all three well up stage.*)

(*flourishes stick and strikes hat-box, which* SPALDING, *who now enters, R., is carrying. Pushes* SPALDING *down stage, upsetting goods and chattels and exit quickly, saying "Pay your debts! Pay your debts!"* HARRY *and* DOUGLAS *laugh loudly. Enter* MRS. STEAD, *R.*)

(*Business of* SPALDING *and* MRS. STEAD *of picking up and redropping props to be humored with audience. Picture at finish of business.*)

MRS. STEAD: (*seeing goods and chattels*) Oh, dear! what a litter! (*runs to assist* SPALDING *in picking them up; he quickly snatches them up and places them on sofa, then sits. To* DOUGLAS) Oh, if you please, sir, this gentleman says—

HARRY: (*crossing to R. door*) Yes, my good woman, this gentleman is going to stay here for a few days.

MRS. STEAD: (*to* DOUGLAS) Mr. Cattermole?

DOUGLAS: (*crossing to c.*) Yes, I am going away for a few days, so please pack my portmanteau.

MRS. STEAD: But, sir, before you go, won't you finish that story?

HARRY: (*at door, impatiently*) Come along, Douglass.

DOUGLAS: Oh, that's soon done. You must know that I've an uncle—

MRS. STEAD: Yes, sir, I know that. Who is very rich.

DOUGLAS: And this uncle has a fixed idea in his head (*crosses to door.*)

HARRY: Come along, Douglas. We shall miss the train.

MRS. STEAD: And what is this idea, sir?

DOUGLAS: In fact, he's a little cracked.

(*Exeunt* DOUGLAS *and* HARRY, *R.*)

MRS. STEAD: Good gracious! here's a discovery! A rich uncle who is a little cracked, (*sees* SPALDING, *bursts out laughing aside; to him*) Oh, I beg your pardon, sir. Are you going to stay here?

SPALDING: I am going to take that liberty if you don't mind. I am to live here.

MRS. STEAD: So Mr. Cattermole says, sir.

SPALDING: But I shall not give you much trouble. Would you kindly tell me where I am to put all my goods and chattels?

MRS. STEAD: Oh certainly, sir. (*running to door, L.*) Here, in this inner room, though both these rooms are at your disposal.

SPALDING: Thanks! (*commences to pick up goods and chattels.*)

MRS. STEAD: (*running across*) Allow me to assist you, sir. (MRS. STEAD *crosses behind sofa to R. of* SPALDING. *At end of business he has the rug between his legs and* MRS. STEAD *follows him holding it up like a train. In front of table she turns to look round to see if anything left, pulling rug tight and tripping* SPALDING *up.*)

(*Attempts to pick up parcels and* SPALDING *hastily snatches them from her. Business ad lib. picking up and dropping parcels etc. then* SPALDING *crosses to L. followed by* MRS. STEAD *laughing; and exit, door L. I. E.*)

MRS. STEAD: (*sinking into chair L. of table*) What a funny little man! Well, at any rate he won't give me much trouble. I think, though, Mr. Cattermole might have asked me if I minded having a stranger staying here, (*knock, R. Packs up cards*) Oh, dear! here's somebody else! Come in! (*knock again*) Another of the creditors, I suppose! Come in! (*third knock*) Oh, come in! (*impatiently*)

Enter CATTERMOLE, *R.; old gentleman; loud voice, gruff, short-spoken.*

CATTERMOLE: Good morning!

(*places hat and stick on sofa*)

MRS. STEAD: Good morning, sir. (*rises, gets L. C.*)

CATTERMOLE: (*coming down*) Does young Mr. Cattermole live here?

MRS. STEAD: Yes, sir, he does.

CATTERMOLE: (*looking about him*) Oh, he does, does he? That's all right!

MRS. STEAD: Yes, sir, but the young gentleman has just gone out.

CATTERMOLE: Oh, he's gone out! Well, so much the better.

MRS. STEAD: But I don't think he'll be very long, sir, because he said—

CATTERMOLE: (*turning sharply on her*) That's quite sufficient! I don't want to hear any more! He's gone out! So you're the old landlady, I suppose?

MRS. STEAD: (*indignantly*) Sir!

CATTERMOLE: (*shouting*) I say you're the old landlady.

MRS. STEAD: (*frightened, goes L., aside*) Oh, what a strange fierce man.

CATTERMOLE: My name's Cattermole.

MRS. STEAD: What, sir?

CATTERMOLE: Watson? No, not Watson! Cattermole! (*spells*) C-a-t-t-e-r-m-o-l-e, mole Cattermole!

MRS. STEAD: (*going L., aside*) Good gracious! it's the cracked uncle! (*in agitation puts hand to face*)

CATTERMOLE: Why, what's the matter with the old fool? What are you crying for?

MRS. STEAD: I'm not crying, sir.

CATTERMOLE: Well, then, don't you laugh at me, don't you laugh at me!

MRS. STEAD: Oh, dear no, sir, I wouldn't think of taking such a liberty.

CATTERMOLE: Well, if you're not laughing or crying, what are you doing? (*loudly*) I say, what are you doing?

MRS. STEAD: (*alarmed*) N—n—nothing, sir.

CATTERMOLE: Yes, you are; you're shaking.

MRS. STEAD: Ah, no, sir; I'm not shaking.

CATTERMOLE: But I say you are!

MRS. STEAD: No, indeed, I am not, sir.

CATTERMOLE: I say you are! (*loudly banging book on table*) And when I say you are you are!

Mrs. Stead: (*meekly*) Yes, sir, I am.

Cattermole: Then what did you say you wasn't for? I know what it is. It's your conscience.

Mrs. Stead: Oh, no, sir.

Cattermole: Yes, it is! Your conscience pricks you.

Mrs. Stead: Oh, no, indeed it does not, sir; my conscience is perfectly clear.

Cattermole: I say it is your conscience! (*loudly with book*) And when I say it is it is.

Mrs. Stead: (*meekly*) Yes, sir, it is.

Cattermole: Then what did you say it wasn't for? I suppose my nephew's a scamp? (*goes c.*)

Mrs. Stead: A scamp, sir?

Cattermole: Yes, a scamp, I said. Don't eat my words! If he is, out with it; don't mind me.

Mrs. Stead: Oh, no, sir! He's the steadiest young man in London.

Cattermole: Steady, is he? (*aside*) Well, I'm very sorry to hear that, (*taking up cards*) Hallo! cards! Does my nephew play cards, eh?

Mrs. Stead: Oh, no, sir, he never touches them!

Cattermole: Never touches them! (*throws down cards disgusted*)

Mrs. Stead: No, sir, it was I playing patience before you came in. (*goes on knees and picks up cards*)

Cattermole: Well, I've no patience with old women playing patience. You ought to be better employed. I'm surprised at you! at your time of life. Well, if he doesn't gamble, what does he do with his time?

Mrs. Stead: (*hesitating*) He

Cattermole: (*loudly*) I say, how does he spend his time? (*stamps*)

Mrs. Stead: He he studies, sir.

Cattermole: Studies? Studies what?

Mrs. Stead: B-b-b-books, sir.

Cattermole: What sorts of b-b-b-books?

Mrs. Stead: All sorts of books, sir.

Cattermole: What sorts of all sorts of books?

Mrs. Stead: (*waves her arms above her head*) All kinds of all sorts of books, sir.

Cattermole (*acknowledging arm waving*) "Oh lor' I thinks she a windmill!"

CATTERMOLE: What kind of all sorts of all—oh, you don't know what you're talking about, (*goes tip to sideboard*) What's this? (*taking up decanter*) What's all this rubbish?

MRS. STEAD: Rubbish, sir! that's not rubbish that's brandy! (*down L.*)

CATTERMOLE: Brandy! (CATTERMOLE *chuckles and says: "Oh! oh!" shaking head reprovingly at* MRS. STEAD *who tosses her head scandalized and indignant*) Oh, well does the boy drink, eh? Does my nephew drink?

MRS. STEAD: Oh, sir, what can have put drink into your head?

CATTERMOLE: No, not into my head, you old fool! I'm talking about my nephew, (*comes down R of table*)

MRS. STEAD: No, sir. He never drinks, never gambles, and likes nothing better than stopping at home and studying.

CATTERMOLE: Has he got any debts?

MRS. STEAD: Oh, no, sir. (*glances aside at bills with a sigh*)

CATTERMOLE: No debts and doesn't drink! Why he must be a perfect ninny! (*goes R. c.*) But, now, tell me what he is like. You see I've been away in India for some years. (MRS. STEAD *says: "Yes, sir," and curtseys.* CATTERMOLE *imitates saying "Well, you needn't say Yes, Sir, as if you knew all about it."*) What is the boy like?

MRS. STEAD: (*going closer to him*) Oh, sir, he is such a handsome young man. (*clasping hands*)

CATTERMOLE: Yes; you old women have such queer tastes. (*imitates*)

MRS. STEAD: And he's so gentle. (*folds hands on breast*)

CATTERMOLE: Oh, gentle! (*imitates*)

MRS. STEAD: And so modest. (*finger of 'R. hand to cheek*)

CATTREMOLE: Oh, modest, is he? (*imitates*)

MRS. STEAD: Oh! oh! oh!

CATTERMOLE: O o oh! sorry to hear that? Well, now tell me how's his liver?

MRS. STEAD: Sir?

CATTERMOLE: (*shouting*) How's his liver?

MRS. STEAD: (*screams and runs to L.*) I do assure you, sir, I've never seen such a thing in the house.

CATTERMOLE: Oh, you're an old fool, you are! (*with shouts of laughter*)

MRS. STEAD: Oh, no, sir I'm not an old fool! Poor dear Stead never called me an old fool.

CATTERMOLE: Well, I'll give you a treat now! (*loudly with book*) I am going to call you an old fool. You're an old fool! And when I say you're an old fool, you are an old fool.

MRS. STEAD: Y y yes, sir, I am,

CATTERMOLE: Then, what did you say you wasn't for? I know all about it, my nephew's an idiot.

MRS. STEAD: Oh, no, indeed, sir. He's very clever.

CATTERMOLE: I say he's an idiot, and if I say he's an idiot, he is an idiot. (*book business*)

MRS. STEAD: Y y yes, sir, he is. (MRS. STEAD *shrieks and collapses on her knees.* CATTERMOLE *stand over her flourishing book*)

CATTERMOLE: Then what did you say he wasn't for? But I'm going to knock all that nonsense out of him! I'll make him sow his wild oats! I'll make him go it.

MRS. STEAD: (*alarmed*) Oh, don't make him go it.

CATTERMOLE: (*determinedly*) I will make him go it.

MRS. STEAD: Oh, please don't make him go it.

CATTERMOLE: He shall go it.

MRS. STEAD: He's getting violent! Oh, do sit down, sir. Pray sit down! (MRS. STEAD *crosses behind table to his right. He says, "Pooh!" at her she retreats up*)

CATTERMOLE: I don't want to sit down, (*sitting R. of table*) I won't sit down! I'll write to the fool. Where are pens, ink and paper? (*takes them in right hand*)

MRS. STEAD: (*Putting writing-case in front of him*) There, sir, you'll find everything there.

CATTERMOLE: I don't want everything! I only want pens, ink and paper. Where's the pen? pen? pen!

MRS. STEAD: There, sir!

CATTERMOLE: (*angrily*) Where? Where?

MRS. STEAD: Why, there, sir, in your hand I That's a pen.

CATTERMOLE: (*seeing it*) Well, I know that, you old stupid, but that isn't the ink, is it?

MRS. STEAD: (*putting inkstand close to his face*) There's the ink, sir.

CATTERMOLE: Well, I don't want to drink it. Where's the note-paper?

MRS. STEAD: (*handing him a packet*) Here's note-paper, lots of note-paper.

CATTERMOLE: (*snatching it from her*) I don't want lots of note-paper. I only want one sheet.

Mrs. Stead: And here are envelopes.

Cattermole: (*snatching them from her and throwing them down, some falling on floor*) Don't play with them.

(Mrs. Stead *picks up envelopes, goes on knees, gathers envelopes, crossing to front of table, drops them again by his feet and makes dives at them with her hand.* Cattermole *draws up legs saying* "Don't you try and tickle me. Go away. What are you digging at? "She says," I'm not digging, sir, I'm picking up the envelopes." *She rises and gets quickly to back of table for blotting paper!*)

Mrs. Stead: There's the blotting paper, (*placing pen in his left hand*) and here's another pen!

Cattermole: I can't write with both hands at once, can I? And now you can go!

Mrs. Stead: But, Mr. Cattermole

Cattermole: You can go! I can write this letter without you.

Mrs. Stead: If you please. Mr. Cattermole, I only just wanted to say one word, (*pointing at him*)

Cattermole: (*interrupting*) But I just don't want you to say it. (*imitates her*)

Mrs. Stead: (*aside, crossing at back to R.*) If I could only speak a good word for his nephew, (*comes to his right*) Mr. Cattermole!

Cattermole: What, ain't you gone yet?

Mrs. Stead: (*running up to door R.*) Oh, I'm going, sir, I'm going!

Cattermole: You're a precious long time about it.

Mrs. Stead: (*coming down a little*) But, Mr. Cattermole.

Cattermole: Oh, she's come back again! Will you go away? Leave me. (*turns his back to her and kicks out*)

Mrs. Stead: But, sir, you haven't seen your nephew for such a long time.

Cattermole: No, and I don't want to see him I'm going to write to the fool.

Mrs. Stead: But if you would only allow me to describe him.

Cattermole: I don't want you to describe him. He's not a panorama, is he?

Mrs. Stead: He's so gentle, and so studious.

Cattermole: Oh dear! oh dear! (*he turns chair round with a howl. She shrieks and runs away*) My good woman, go and play! go and run up and down!

Mrs. Stead: And he never goes out always, etc. etc.

CATTERMOLE: (*buries his head in his hands, then takes piece of blotting paper and gives it to her*) Here's some paper! Go and blot yourself out altogether!

MRS. STEAD: Oh! (*Exit R., hurriedly*)

CATTERMOLE: I believe she'd have stayed here all day if I'd encouraged her! that I do. Now, if she'd told me that my nephew was fast, had a lot of gay companions, and, in fact, was a regular little demon, I believe I could have cuddled that old woman. But I won't cuddle her. I'll write to the fool!

(*turns to write*)

(*Enter SPALDING, L. Umbrella in left hand, hat on handkerchief in right hand. He carefully closes door after him, and walks across at back to R. c. As he enters CATTERMOLE looks up t sees him and whistles in astonishment.*)

CATTERMOLE: (*rising and going round at back to him*) This is the young hopeful I suppose! (*as they meet, R. c., SPALDING looks up, sees him, and turns to walk back again*) Come here! (SPALDING *stops near door L. Shouting*) Come here!! (SPALDING *turns*) Sit down! (SPALDING *hesitates*) Sit down!! (SPALDING *places umbrella by door and is going to sit on chair placed there*) No, not there, here, here! Come and sit down here! (*throws book on chair, L. of table. SPALDING walks nervously to chair and sits*) Take that hat off. (CATTERMOLE *says, "Oh, lor'!" averts face, extends left arm, waves hand,* SPALDING *nervously shakes hands.* CATTERMOLE *knocks hand away with a grol.* SPALDING *does so and looks at him, smooths hair.* CATTERMOLE *sits; looking at him*) Oh! oh! oh! (*bursts into a fit of laughter*) What a face! (SPALDING *rubs his nose with handkerchief rolled up tight. Knocking his hand down*) Don't do that when I'm talking to you. (SPALDING *looks at him bewildered*) He looks like a parson, I'm blest if he don't! (*repeat handkerchief business*) Don't do that! (SPALDING *makes for door, L., and goes off.* CATTERMOLE *follows, drags him back, and throws him into chair.* CATTERMOLE *stands over him gives him three vicious punches.* SPALDING *squirms and finally falls on floor—Picture*) How dare you run away when I'm talking to you? (*going round back of table to his seat*) You're a perfect young fiend, you are! (*sees blue ribbon in* SPALDING's *coat*) Hallo! What's this? (*pointing to ribbon* SPALDING *puts hand up.* CATTERMOLE *taps it with pen*) No, not that! this! this! this! (*pulling coat and hauling him half over table*) What do you want to wear that for now? The boat race is all over long ago. (SPALDING *again looks at him, bewildered*) Oh, oh, oh!

(*aside*) And that's the heap of misery that old fool of a woman called handsome! handsome that is! let's have a look at Handsome, (*puts glasses on and looks at him*)

SPALDING: I've no doubt you are surprised! (CATTERMOLE *shouts with laughter*)

CATTERMOLE: Surprised! surprised! I should think I was surprised for of all the objects (*repeat handkerchief business*) Don't do that! (CATTERMOLE *knocks it out of his hand.* SPALDING *goes and picks it up.* CATTERMOLE *sees goloshes*) Hallo! What are those? What on earth have you got on your feet? What are those? (*tapping goloshes with pen*)

SPALDING: Those are my goloshes.

CATTERMOLE: Go what?

SPALDING: Goloshes!

GATTERMOLE: Goloshes! What do you want to wear goloshes for?

SPALDING: D' you know

CATTERMOLE: (*shouting and bringing his hand down on table*) No, I don't know! (*run off. repeat business making for door, etc.*) How dare you run away when I'm talking to you? I want to talk to you calmly and quietly. Now, then, what do you want to wear those wretched things for?

SPALDING: D' you know (*catches* CATTERMOLE's *eye attempts to run off.* CATTERMOLE *says "No you don't," and stops him*)

CATTERMOLE: No, I don't

SPALDING: I wear these because I'm so used to them.

CATTERMOLE: Oh, you want to slink about like a ghost, I suppose.

SPALDING: No.

CATTERMOLE: Yes, you do!

SPALDING: Yes.

CATTERMOLE: (*mocking*) Yes. Then what do you want to wear them for?

SPALDING: I suffer so much with chronic influenza,

CATTERMOLE: Oh, you do? Well, that's all right! Now tell me. How's your liver?

SPALDING: How's what?

CATTERMOLE: (*gruffly*) How's your liver!

SPALDING: Nicely, thanks. (CATTERMOLE *laughs*)

CATTERMOLE: Oh, that's all right.

SPALDING: How's yours?

CATTERMOLE: (*angrily, rising.* SPALDING *nearly falls off chair*) Never you mind my liver; you look after your own that's quite enough for you to do. Now, what do you want to wear those Indian liver, I mean india-rubber things for?

SPALDING: I wear them to keep my feet warm while walking.

CATTERMOLE: Walking! But what do you want to walk for? (SPALDING *says "H'm?"* CATTERMOLE *mimicks*) What on earth do you want to walk at all for?

SPALDING: Because I can't afford to ride

CATTERMOLE: Can't afford to ride. Why not?

SPALDING: D' you know

CATTERMOLE: (*shouting*) No. I don't know! If I knew I shouldn't ask you you idiot!

SPALDING: No! You see the London cabmen use such bad language.

CATTERMOLE: Yes that's their livers.

SPALDING: And they're so extortionate in their charges.

CATTERMOLE: I say that doesn't affect you. You have an uncle, you have a rich uncle, you have a wealthy (*disgusted at* SPALDING's *not understanding*) Oh! you have an uncle, damn it!

SPALDING: I have an uncle Robert.

CATTERMOLE: (*turns away from him*) Oh, dear! oh, dear! oh, dear! (*to him*) Now, listen to me. Everybody (*handkerchief business as before*) Don't do that! Put that thing away. Don't let me see it again! (SPALDING *puts handkerchief in pocket*) Everybody makes fools of themselves some time or other. (SPALDING *says "M' yes!"* CATTERMOLE *says "Eh? oh! yes"*) When it's done young it doesn't matter they improve as they grow older, but there are no fools like old fools.

SPALDING: Yes.

CATTERMOLE: But I say there are not!

SPALDING: Ye-es.

CATTERMOLE: I say there are not! There are no fools like old fools. (*threatening him with book*)

SPALDING: Oh, no! there are no fools like old fools. (*pointedly*)

CATTERMOLE: I'm determined you shan't be one of the latter. You understand that? (SPALDING *starts to say "No."* CATTERMOLE *threatens him and corrects himself to "Yes" hastily*)

SPALDING: Yes. I understand that.

CATTERMOLE: I'm glad of that. Because I'd rather strangle you with my own hands—that I would.

SPALDING: How nice!

CATTERMOLE: (*turning from him disgusted*) How nice! I wonder if the poor fool's hard up? I suppose I'd better give him some money.

(SPALDING *takes off golosh*)

CATTERMOLE: (*to* SPALDING) Here, give me your purse.

SPALDING: H'm?

(SPALDING *looks at him suspiciously*)

CATTERMOLE: (*determinedly*) Hand me over your purse!

SPALDING: (*rising*) No.

(*Runs over at back to door, R., crying "Help, help!" followed by* CATTERMOLE. *Enter* MRS. STEAD, *R.* SPALDING *puts her in front of him;* CATTERMOLE *jams them both behind door, shaking his fist at* SPALDING; MRS. STEAD *screams;* CATTERMOLE *gets his stick.*)

MRS. STEAD: Oh, don't strike him, sir, please don't strike him.

CATTERMOLE: Don't cuddle me, old woman! (*taking up hat*) I shall come back, and I'll make him go it; if I don't I'm—(*strikes door with stick and exits, furious.* MRS. STEAD *closes doors, goes c. showing* SPALDING *on knees hiding behind the window curtain. He rises and gets c. to catch her*)

MRS. STEAD: (*falling into* SPALDING's *arms*) Oh. sir, I can't stand it. I am going to faint. (SPALDING *fans her with golosh*)

MRS. STEAD: He's mad, sir. I'm sure he's mad.

SPALDING: (*going to L. of table*) Do you know, I think the poor old gentleman's a lunatic he wanted my purse.

MRS. STEAD: Did he indeed, sir? How alarmed you must have been. You're looking quite pale. Sit down and I'll make you a nice cup of tea.

(*crosses at back to door,* SPALDING *sits L of table*)

(*Enter* GIBSON, *R., showing in* KNOX *with writ*)

GIBSON: Serve the writ on him! I'll teach him to say I'm no gentleman; confound his impertinence!

(*Places stick on sofa.* KNOX *crosses to* SPALDING, *slaps him heavily on shoulder and places writ in his hand*)

SPALDING: What is this?

KNOX: A writ.

(*Exit. R.* SPALDING *reads writ, bewildered*)

GIBSON: (*crossing to* SPALDING) Now, which is the gentleman? (*seeing* SPALDING) Why, it's the wrong man!

MRS. STEAD: Who is it you want, sir? (*at door R.*)

GIBSON: Mr. Marsland.

MRS. STEAD: Oh, sir; he's just gone out of town with Mr. Cattermole.

GIBSON: Out of town! Where's he gone to?

MRS. STEAD: I don't know, sir; somewhere in the country.

GIBSON: Oh, I know. He's gone home! Here, fetch me a cab.

MRS. STEAD: Yes, sir. (*Exit door R.*)

GIBSON: I'll be on their track before (*feeling in pocket*) Why, hang it all, I haven't got any change, (*sees* SPALDING; *goes to him*) Here, lend me a sovereign.

SPALDING: (*terrified*) No.

(*Rises and turns to run round at lack to R. door.* GIBSON *goes to meet him, turning over chair, R.* SPALDING *avoids* GIBSON *by turning and crossing, front to R. door, leaping overturned chair and crying, "Help, help!" followed by* GIBSON, *calling, "Where are you going to?" etc.* SPALDING *tries to open door, R., but cannot do so; then jumps through window.* GIBSON *seizes by leg and calling, "Help, help!"*)

CURTAIN.

Act II

SCENE. *Morning-room at* MR. MARSLAND'S *country house; doors R. i E., R. U. E., L. i E., L. U. E.; casement window, C., opening on to conservatory; fireplace, R.; piano, L.; hunting portraits and trophies on walls; large oak chest at back, L. Miss* ASH FORD *discovered seated at table R., reading book.*

MISS ASHFORD: It's as plain as the sun at noonday. Besides, what rapid strides Spiritualism has made during the last few years! Ah, if I could but convince Mr. Marsland of the reality of the spirits! Why, here it says they may even be photographed by the aid of a medium, (*rising and going up to c.*) Now where are those girls? They've sneaked off again; they always do directly I begin to read. Oh, there they stand looking down the road through a glass, (*looks off to L.*)

(*Enter* MR. MARSLAND, *L. i E.*)

MISS ASHFORD: (*calling*) My dears! my dears! that is very unbecoming most unladylike.

MARSLAND: What! Are the girls disobeying again?

(*looks off. to L.*)

MISS ASHFORD: Well, judge for yourself, Mr. Marsland. There's your daughter climbing up a huge heap of stones.

MARSLAND: Oh, come now, there's nothing very disgraceful in that.

MISS ASHFORD: (*coming down, R.*) No, but it's such bad form.

MARSLAND: (*coming down, c.*) Well, just now there's no one to see them, (*motions Miss* ASHFORD *to seat and sits on settee*) You know I'm rather glad I've found you alone, for the fact is, I shall be so busy hunting the next few days that I shall have no time for the girls.

MISS ASHFORD: Well, am I not here?

MARSLAND: Yes, and you know my rules, no flirtation.

MISS ASHFORD: Oh, you may depend upon me. I'll keep the girls occupied. Besides they can have some music with the new private secretary. You know he's very musical.

MARSLAND: Yes. I hope he'll improve their music. But you know, the song he sang last night was scarcely the style of music I expected.

MISS ASHFORD: Indeed? What was it?

MARSLAND: Yes. Let me see, you saw nothing of him last night.

Miss Ashford: No. I was so ill I was obliged to keep to my room.

Marsland: Oh, yes, I remember. Well then, the song he sang. . . Bless me if I can remember. Oh, yes, the song he sang was something like this, (*substitute title of latest well-known comic song*) Do you like that style?

Miss Ashford: Not much I But I daresay it's from one of the oratorios. You know I take a great interest in the dear boy on account of my long friendship with his mother. I hope he'll be happy here.

Marsland: Yes, but you must not make too much fuss with the young fellow. You must remember that he is in a subordinate position, and must be kept within his proper sphere.

Miss Ashford: Oh, I daresay his mental culture is quite equivalent to our social position. Besides, I never can forget my lifelong friendship with his mother. (*rising and giving book to him*) But to change the subject, will you allow me to persuade you to read that book?

Marsland: (*rising and looking at book*) "The Latest Proof of Spiritualism." Bah I don't come near me with such nonsense. (*goes L.*)

Miss Ashford: Oh, if I had a medium I could Soon convince you.

Maryland: My dear Miss Ashford, go in for all that sort of humbug (Edith *and* Eva *heard laughing and talking without*) as much as you please, but don't you put such stuff into my daughter's head.

Miss Ashford: Certainly not; but its not nonsense! (*goes up R.*)

(*Enter* Edith *and* Eva, *running and laughing, c. from L.* Edith *with dog-whip, runs down R. of* Marsland. Eva, *with glasses, hands them to Miss* Ashford, *and remains up stage with her, over R.*)

Marsland: (*taking* Edith's *hands*) Why, what on earth is the matter?

Edith: Oh, papa, there's a cab coming, with such a fat old gentleman in it.

Eva: Yes, we saw him quite plainly.

Marsland: Well, did you never see a fat old gentleman before? (Edith *says "Not fatter than you. He's just like a mountain with the setting sun on top."*) I was just going to speak to you upon the subject. Here, Eva, come here I (Eva *come down, L. C. both girls keep up a constant chatter*) Quiet, quiet! Will you be (*they cease talking*) Mr. Spalding has been very highly recommended to me, so you must not play him any of your pranks, as you did his predecessor.

　　　　　　　　　　　　　　　　　CHARLES HAWTREY

EDITH: Oh, papa, we never did.

EVA: No, we never did.

MARSLAND: (*putting his arms on their shoulders*) Oh come now we know all about that. You must remember that you are grown up now, and must drop all your practical jokes. (EVA *tries to snatch dog-whip from* EDITH. *Girls dispute saying, "Let me have it," "No, it's my own whip," etc., etc.*) Now! now! now! Mr. Spalding is a very talented man, and it's a great chance for you to reap some advantage from his presence amongst us. So mind you treat him with respect, and at the same time make him feel at home.

EDITH & EVA: (*together*) Yes. Certainly.

MARSLAND: But you must promise me that!

EVA & EDITH (*together*) We promise!

(*noise of cab starts off*)

MARSLAND: Very well, then on that condition I forgive all past sins, (*listening*) Hallo! why that must be the carriage with the stout party you spoke of. (*goes up, c.* EDITH *goes up R.* EVA *runs up after* MARSLAND, *and jumps up to look over his shoulder, jumps on chair R. of opening, hand on* MARSLAND's *shoulder. As he exits she nearly falls off chair laughs*) I wonder who it can be?

(*Exit, c. to L.*)

MISS ASHFORD: (*coming down c.* EVA *comes down L.*) There, young ladies, you heard what papa said. Now, how often have I warned and entreated you?

EDITH: Ah, but you were amused yourself.

MISS ASHFORD: But in this instance I shall be against you throughout, for this young man is the son of my oldest and dearest friend.

EVA: Well, you should have seen us with him last night. (EDITH *above* MISS ASHFORD *shakes head.* EVA *catches her eye and changes to very demure tone*) I'm sure our conduct was most discreet.

MISS ASHFORD: (*to* EDITH) And yours?

EDITH: Most! (*very demurely*)

MISS ASHFORD: I should like to have seen that.

EDITH: but he's not a bit like your description of him.

MISS ASHFORD: My dear, mine was only a fancy portrait, for I only saw him once, when he was a tiny little baby. Now, he may be an Apollo, or the reverse, for anything I know, but he must have a sweet face has he not?

EDITH: Yes, he is rather nice looking.

EVA: (*crossing to R.*) And plays a rattling good game at billiards.

MRS ASHFORD: Eva, my dear!

EVA: Well, that's what cousin Harry says.

(*Enter* MARSLAND *and* CATTERMOLE, *c. from L.*)

MARSLAND: (*L. c.*) Ah, my dear old friend, this is indeed an unexpected pleasure.

CATTERMOLE: (*c.*) Yes, I could not stay away when once I returned.

MARSLAND: (*introducing*) This is Miss Ashford, Mr. Cattermole.

CATTERMOLE: (*going to* EDITH *who comes down R. c.*) How do you do, Miss Ashford?

EDITH: (*laughing*) I am not Miss Ashford.

CATTERMOLE: Then where is Miss Ashford? (*turning*)

MISS ASHFORD: I am Miss Ashford. (*comes down R. c.*)

CATTERMOLE: (*shaking hands*) Oh, how do you do?

MISS ASHFORD: Happy to know you, Mr. Scaffoldpole.

CATTERMOLE: No, Cattermole! (*spells*)

MARSLAND: This is my daughter Edith.

CATTERMOLE: (*shaking hands*) How do you do, Miss Edith? I hope we shall be good friends.

EDITH: Yes, I hope so.

MARSLAND: Why, of course you will.

EDITH: This is my friend, Eva Webster.

CATTERMOLE: How do you do, Miss Webster? hope you're better. (EDITH *and* EVA *at fireplace,* MARSLAND *sits on settee L. c.* EVA *bursts out laughing, goes up and sits in armchair.* MARSLAND *looks at her reprovingly; to* MARSLAND) Miss Webster's a bit of a kitten, isn't she?

MISS ASHFORD: I was about to ask you, Mr. Rattlepole

CATTERMOLE: Cattermole! (*spells*)

MISS ASHFORD: I was about to ask you if you believe in spirits?

CATTERMOLE: Spirits! Well, yes in moderation.

MISS ASHFORD: Don't you think they influence our lives for good?

CATTERMOLE: Yes. I shouldn't go in for them too much if I were you.

MISS ASHFORD: Not too much? Oh if I had my own way I would devote my entire life to them.

CATTERMOLE: What a bibulous old lady to be sure.

MARSLAND: I say, Miss Ashford, you must keep your Spiritualistic craze within reasonable bounds.

MISS ASHFORD: So I do.

MARSLAND: Would you mind letting us have a little luncheon here and seeing after Mr. Cattermole's room?

MISS ASHFORD: With great pleasure.

MARSLAND: Thanks!

(*sits with* CATTERMOLE *on settee*)

MISS ASHFORD: Come along, young ladies. (CATTERMOLE *is blowing kisses to girls, as Miss* ASHFORD *up, she sees him is scandalized. Exit, R. u. E.*)

EVA: (*to* EDITH *as they go up*) Why, Edith dear, you are always so cold to strangers. You behave quite differently to him.

EDITH: Yes, he's an old fellow (EDITH *swings* EVA *across to L. c. She falls on one knee at* CATERMOLES *feet and looks up at him coquettishly.* CATTERMOLE *pleased*) and I always respect age.

EVA: And size! (*laughs. Exeunt, R. u. E.*)

CATTERMOLE: That's a very nice girl your daughter.

(CATTERMOLE *on R. of settee,* MARSLAND *on L. of settee*)

MARSLAND: Yes, and she's a good girl, too.

CATTERMOLE: You won't have her at home long.

MARSLAND: Eh why why?

CATTERMOLE: Why why

MARSLAND: Oh, she's a perfect child yet.

CATTERMOLE: Yes, they're the sort of children that are run after.

MARSLAND: She mustn't think of that sort of thing for another three years at least.

CATTERMOLE: Oh, you give her three years, do you, well, I don't! But tell me now how's her liver?

MARSLAND: Eh?

CATTERMOLE: How's her liver, I said.

MARSLAND: (*laughing*) Why she hasn't got a liver yet.

CATTERMOLE: Hasn't she? What a lucky state of things. I wish I hadn't, but I have, and well I know it.

MARSLAND: Suppose we change the subject.

CATTERMOLE: I wish you could change my liver.

MARSLAND: How about that old scheme of ours that your nephew should marry Edith?

CATTERMOLE: (*uneasily*) My nephew?

MARSLAND: Yes, your nephew?

CATTERMOLE: Oh, you mean my nephew oh, of course. Well you know I think we'd better forget all about that.

MARSLAND: Forget all about it! (CATTERMOLE *says Ye es!*) Why, you wrote to me about nothing else, from India.

CATTERMOLE: From India, yes.

MARSLAND: Don't you remember, not three months ago, describing the sort of young fellow that you hoped to find him?

CATTERMOLE: That I hoped to find him ye es.

MARSLAND: Have you seen him?

CATTERMOLE: Yes; I've seen him! Oh, don't! please don't!

MARSLAND: Does he come up to your expectations?

CATTERMOLE: Up to them. He's far, far beyond them.

MARSLAND: Aren't you satisfied with him?

CATTERMOLE: Satisfied with him? Why he hasn't made the slightest endeavor to carry out one of my wishes. He's a ninny! a nincompoop!

MARSLAND: I'm sorry to hear that.

CATTERMOLE: He's got a blue ribbon thing here.

(*pointing to button-hole*)

MARSLAND: A blue ribbon!

CATTERMOLE: And wears goloshes; My nephew wears goloshes!

MARSLAND: Goloshes! I never heard of such a thing.

CATTERMOLE No. nor! in the whole course of my life!

MARSLAND: Well, perhaps the poor fellow's delicate,

CATTERMOLE: He's no right to be delicate, has he? I'm not delicate, am I? (*rises*)

MARSLAND: (*smiling*) No.

CATTERMOLE: I should think not, indeed. If I had I should have been dead years ago. I say, do you remember the night I drove the costermonger's cart from Covent Garden to St. John's Wood in the pouring rain?

(*sits again*)

MARSLAND: Yes, I remember.

CATTERMOLE: What a night that was. Shall you ever forget it?

MARSLAND: Never.

CATTERMOLE: I say, you were getting on a bit that night, weren't you?

MARSLAND: (*uneasily*) No.

CATTERMOLE: Don't you remember we'd been to Evans (*singing*) "Oh, who will o'er the downs so free, To win a bloo" (MARSLAND *stops* CATTERMOLE) What's the matter?

MARSLAND: (*looking around uneasily*) I say, we can't have anything bloo here now, you know; you must remember that all this happened years and years ago.

CATTERMOLE: Yes, that must be five-and-twenty years ago. I was a little slim chap then; wasn't I?

MARSLAND: Ah, so you were.

CATTERMOLE: Do you remember the night I tried to crawl through the railings in Hyde Park?

MARSLAND: No, I don't think I remember anything about that.

CATTERMOLE: Why, you were with us that night you must remember.

MARSLAND: No I don't seem to.

CATTERMOLE: Oh, no, of course not, you were run in. (*laughs*)

MARSLAND: Oh, no! no!

(*looking round uneasily*)

CATTERMOLE: Yes; don't you remember you wanted to take the policeman to your club?

MARSLAND: (*trying to silence him*) Nothing of that kind tell me

CATTERMOLE: I shall never forget your struggling to get a light from his bull's-eye.

MARSLAND: Never mind his bull's-eye. Tell me something about your nephew.

CATTERMOLE: I never shall forget that night as long; as I live.

MARSLAND: Your nephew! Your nephew!

CATTERMOLE: (*stops laughing*) Eh? Oh, no, don't let's talk about him. He's a failure, a downright failure.

HARRY: (*off c.*) Come along, Spalding!

(*Enter* DOUGLAS *and* HARRY*, c. from L. Enter* JOHN *with luncheon , R. u. E. He lays same on table, R., and exits L. u. E.* DOUGLAS *goes down to L. corner.* HARRY *to R. C.* MARSLAND *remains on settee*)

MARSLAND: (*to* DOUGLAS) Ah, Mr. Spalding, here you are at last. I must ask you to be a little earlier in your hour of rising in the future, (*introducing* HARRY *who is down R.*) This is my nephew Harry.

CATTERMOLE: (*shaking hands*) How do you do Harry? (*rises, goes R.*)

HARRY: How do you do? (*goes to fireplace*)

CATTERMOLE: (*to* MARSLAND) Why, he looks quite the pink of perfection, doesn't he? When I look at him, and think of that miserable object of mine oh!

MARSLAND: Mr. Spalding, Mr. Cattermole.

(DOUGLAS *starts and stares at* CATTERMOLE)

CATTERMOLE: Well, what are you staring at? Did you never hear the name Cattermole before? (CATTERMOLE *intones as he spells it and sits at table*)

DOUGLAS: Yes, I know how to spell it.

(*goes up to* HARRY)

MARSLAND: (*sitting on settee*) You know, Mr. Spalding, I'm so very pleased the young ladies are to have the benefit of your highly cultivated literary tastes. (*with paper, not seeing* DOUGLAS *go up*)

(DOUGLAS *and* HARRY *express in dumb show, their surprise and amusement at having met* MR. CATTERMOLE. HARRY *puffs out cheek and with hands passing over stomach indicates* CATTERMOLE'S *size.* DOUGLAS *laughs and slaps thigh, drawing* MARSLAND'S *attention to him.* DOUGLAS, *who is laughing, catches* MARSLAND'S *eye, subsides and returns to L. corner*)

MARSLAND: First of all (*turning, and seeing* DOUGLAS) Mr. Spalding, I must ask for a little of your attention, if you please. I was saying that first of all I am going to ask you to give them a few lessons.

DOUGLAS: Lessons?

MARSLAND: Yes read with them interest them, and so forth,

DOUGLAS: I'll do my best to interest them.

CATTERMOLE: Yes, you look quite capable.

(*shakes finger at* DOUGLAS)

MARSLAND: And, then, I'm going to ask you to give them some music.

DOUGLAS: Music? (*nonplussed*)

MARSLAND: Yes. I'm so very glad you're musical.

DOUGLAS: (*confused*) Oh, yes; so I am!

(DOUGLAS *goes c. to* HARRY *in alarm then crosses to top of table for pie bus.*)

CATTERMOLE: (*to* MARSLAND) I say, old fellow, this is a capital pie.

MARSLAND: Is it?

CATTERMOLE: Um!

MARSLAND: I'm glad you like it.

CATTERMOLE: Yes, there's only one thing wanting.

MARSLAND: Eh?

CATTERMOLE: I say there's only one thing wanting in that pie, and that is

DOUGLAS: (*interrupting*) Mushrooms! (*attabli*)

CATTERMOLE: I beg your pardon.

DOUGLAS: Mushrooms!

CATTERMOLE: Mushrooms? (*looking about*) I don't see any. Where are they?

DOUGLAS: (*taking up fork, and emphasizijig by tapping pie with it*) No, no, you misunderstand me. I thought you said there was one thing wanting in the pie.

CATTERMOLE: (*waving off* DOUGLAS' *fork*) Yes, I did say that.

DOUGLAS: I merely suggested mushrooms. It's the one thing wanting to give it a flavor.

MARSLAND: (*to* CATTERMOLE) By Jove, he's right there, though!

CATTERMOLE: (*hitting at* DOUGLAS' *fork*) Oh, yes, he's quite right (*to* DOUGLAS) but I wouldn't fork it about quite so much as that if I were you.

DOUGLAS: Now you know, there are precious few cooks who know how to do the thing really smartly.

CATTERMOLE: Is that so? (*repeats fork bus.*)

DOUGLAS: Now the best place in town to get a thing of this kind really good is at the Continental, (*stops short and drops fork,* CATTERMOLE *and* MARSLAND *stare*) On—on the Continent.

CATTERMOLE: That's the first time I ever heard the Continent was in town, (*to* MARSLAND) I say, old man, do you remember when we went on the Continent together? What games we had. Harry come here! (*whispers him.* DOUGLAS *looks knowingly at* MARSLAND *and imitates the can-fan.* MARSLAND *laughs then pulls up shocked.* DOUGLAS *recollecting turns up c.* CATTERMOLE *looks at* MARSLAND *and says; "Oh you gay old cock, you!"* MARSLAND *looks disconcerted; all laugh;* MARSLAND *looks at* DOUGLAS; *pulls him Up*)

CATTERMOLE: (*to* DOUGLAS) Where did you pick up your Continental experience, young fellow?

DOUGLAS: Oh I used to go there every evening
(*sees mistake*)

MARSLAND: (*astonished*) Every eve? And where have you gained your culinary knowledge?

DOUGLAS: I—I've an uncle, who's a cook, (*leaning over settee*) A damned good cook too!
(*slaps* MARSLAND *on shoulder*)

(MARSLAND *starts up.* CATTERMOLE, *who is drinking a glass of wine & chokes, and spits it out on carpet. He beats his back, shakes his fist at* DOUGLAS,/<?2/r.r *out another glass of wine, drinks it and falls back in his chair exhausted.* HARRY *pats* CATTERMOLE's *back goes up to* DOUGLAS *and remonstrates in dumb show*)

MARSLAND: Mr. Spalding, I must ask you to be kind enough to moderate your language.

DOUGLAS: (*looks at* HARRY, *who prompts him to say*) Merely a manner of speaking, you know.

(HARRY *and* DOUGLAS *go up to c. opening.* MARSLAND *crosses to* CATTERMOLE)

MARSLAND: I should rather think it was. (*to* CATTERMOLE) Well, how about the pie? Have you enjoyed it? (CATTERMOLE *nods assent*) Better? (CAT-TERMOLE *nods assent*) Well, as soon as you're quite recovered 1 should like to show you my horses.

CATTERMOLE: Yes, you'll give me no peace till you do will you?

MARSLAND: And after that if you feel inclined we'll have a look over the kennels.

CATTERMOLE: Yes, we generally end by going to the dogs. (*rises*)

DOUGLAS: (*running down R. c. and slapping* MARSLAND *on the back*) Shall I come too?

MARSLAND: (*with dignity*) You come, too? My dear sir, you have your duties to attend to!

(*cross and exit, R. i E.*)

CATTERMOLE: (*to* DOUGLAS) Yes, you'll go to the dogs quite soon enough.

(*Exit, following* MARSLAND)

HARRY: I say, Douglas, you really must be more careful, you're certain to be found out if you're not.

DOUGLAS: I can't help it, old fellow, I'm getting reckless and beginning to go it.

(*Enter* JOHN, *L. u. E.*)

HARRY: But you shouldn't tell people that you go to the Continental every evening.

JOHN: Beg pardon, sir, there's a gentleman wishes to see you.

HARRY: Who me?

JOHN: Yes, sir. (DOUGLAS *turns up to piano*)

HARRY: What's his name?

JOHN: He wouldn't say, sir.

HARRY: What's his business?

JOHN: I don't know, sir. He said he wouldn't detain you a moment, but that his business was most im- portant.

HARRY: Very well, I'll go to him at once. I won't be long, Douglas.
(*Exit, L. u. E.*)

(JOHN *crosses to table R. c.; and exits, R. i E., carrying tray and table as it stands.*)

DOUGLAS: All right, old chap! I rather like this place, (*at piano', taking up photos of girls*) The old boy does the thing well, and these little girls are simply delightful. (*goes down in front of settee*)

(*Enter Miss* ASHFORD, *c. from R.*)

MISS ASHFORD: (*aside*) There he is. He shall find a second mother in me! I never thought he would have grown so tall.

(DOUGLAS *kisses photos and sits.*)

MISS ASHFORD: My dear Robert (*kisses him. He crosses again to L. astonished. He runs to door L. i E. and turns hiding photos behind him, replaces photos on piano hastily as she turns her back*) Don't seek to run away! It was but a motherly embrace. I will explain. I was your mother's dearest friend, and was introduced to you when you were only two months old and about so high. (*hands near ground*)

DOUGLAS I really don't remember.

MISS ASHFORD: Naturally; but I do, and you were such a tiny lump of pink soft terra cotta, with flaxen hair.

DOUGLAS: Flaxen hair? Do you mean to say that my hair was ever flaxen?

MISS ASHFORD: Yes, when you were a baby and curly.

DOUGLAS: Oh, yes of course. But then one's hair grows darker as one grows older.

MISS ASHFORD: Not always, as you may find if you live long enough, (*points to her own hair*) But now let me look at you, and see if you resemble your dear mother at all. (*puts on spectacles; he leans over settee*) Not a bit; not an atom! She was very handsome. (DOUGLAS *laughs, gets L. c. Goes and sits, R. c.*)

DOUGLAS: Oh, I'm like my father; you know it's the case sometimes.

MISS ASHFORD: Well, whoever you are like, I am heartily glad to have you here. My heart jumped for joy when I saw your testimonials.

DOUGLAS: My testimonials were good?

MISS ASHFORD: Excellent! Especially the one for classical music.

DOUGLAS: Yes, I thought that would be good.
(*sits on settee*)

MISS ASHFORD: You must have worked very hard.

DOUGLAS: Yes, I took a deal of trouble.

Miss Ashford: Well, I think you'll be happy here.

Douglas: I hope so.

Miss Ashford: Mr, Marsland is a nice kind gentleman, very fond of good music. Miss Edith is a little too fond of fun and frolic, but she's a very good girl for all that

Douglas: But there was another Eva.

Miss Ashford: Yes. Edith being alone, Mr. Marsland invited the daughter of a friend of his to live in the house. Oh, she's a darling child.

Douglas: (*drily*) Yes, they both seem darling children.

Miss Ashford: Yes, they are very good girls, but full of their tricks. You mustn't let them impose upon you too much.

Douglas: Oh, never fear; I shall know how to make use of my authority. Besides, my reception was most cordial. They were most kind.

Miss Ashford: Ah, that was my doing. In fact, you must depend upon me for everything in this house. If you have a favorite dish or anything of that kind let me know, and I will see to it for you.

Douglas: Very kind of you, I'm sure.

Miss Ashford: (*going to him and suddenly grasping his wrist. He rises*) But there's one thing, my dear Robert, I want you to do for me. (*looks around mysteriotisly, he does same. Both turning together they bump back to back*) I want you I want you to get me some books on Spiritualism for the library. Will you?

Douglas: Oh, is Mr. Marsland a Spiritualist?

Miss Ashford: Oh dear no, I wish he was, but I am. I am devoted to the science, (*turning to him and making a sudden pass, he retreats alarmed. She makes several passes. He retreats alarmed to door L. i E. watches her and then makes semi-burlesque imitations of her gestures*) Are you initiated? Are you one of us?

(*up c.*)

Douglas: I really don't know but I've heard a great deal about it. (*back of settee*)

Miss Ashford: Oh, you do know something about it. That's all right. Then this evening we'll take a walk together.

Douglas: (*aside*) Oh, will we?

Miss Ashford: We'll have a conference, and exchange views.

Douglas: Yes. I wouldn't miss that for the world.

(*goes up c.*)

Miss Ashford: But now I must leave you, for I have a hundred things to see to. It is not necessary that everybody should know on what intimate terms we are.

Douglas: Certainly not. I am happy to have found so good a friend. (*kisses her hand, goes up L.*)

Miss Ashford: Now, no formality, my dear Robert, but come to my heart, where the memory of your dear mother dwells, (*he goes to her embraces awkwardly: going up*) And now, good-bye, my dear Robert, and remember that you are to look upon this house as your home, and upon me as your second mother.

(*Exit, R. u. E.*)

Douglas: (*coming down, R.*) What a remarkable old lady! Funny household altogether! (*He puts chair which was by table R. c. above door R. i E.*) Anyhow the existence of Edith and Eva reconciles me to the place

(*Enter* Harry, *quickly, c. from L.*)

Harry: I say, Douglas, here's the devil to pay. Gibson's here and swears he won't go until he's paid.

Douglas: But what did you say?

Harry: I didn't say anything. I couldn't pay the man. (*goes L.*)

(*Enter* Gibson, *c. from L.*)

Gibson: Ah! good morning, gentlemen.

Douglas: I say, Gibson, what cheek! What do you want here? (*R.*)

Gibson: (*c. to* Harry) You sent your hunting coat to be repaired. I remembered it, sent it down, and took the liberty of following it.

Douglas: But what for?

Gibson: He owes Mr. Jenkins three hundred pounds for a bill due four days ago.

Douglas: But what s that got to do with you?

Gibson: I've bought that bill and want to know if he's ready to pay.

(Douglas *looks at* Harry *amused*)

Harry: (*leaning over settee*) We shall soon be returning to town, Mr. Gibson; when everything shall be made straight

Douglas: Yes, the very moment we arrive

Gibson: Very likely, but I want it made straight here and now.

Harry: Oh, that's impossible!

Marsland: (*without*) All right I'll see about it.

(*off, i E.*)

GIBSON: (*crossing to R.*) Impossible? How would you like the writ shown to your uncle?

DOUGLAS: Let's kick him out of the house.

(*crosses L. above settee*)

HARRY: That would be no good. We must keep him quiet somehow, (*crossing to* GIBSON. HARRY *crosses below settee*) Look here, Gibson, I'm sure you will listen to reason. Can't this thing be arranged?

GIBSON: Yes, sir, it can in one way.

HARRY: What is that?

GIBSON: By letting me remain down here with you.

HARRY: Oh, that's impossible!

GIBSON: Oh, don't say that, sir. Do you know it's the ambition of my life to be invited on a visit to a Country mansion?

HARRY: But, my uncle, the guests?

GIBSON: Oh, bless your soul, I shan't disgrace you. I can behave like a gentleman if I like. Now, you must arrange this for me.

MARSLAND: (*without*) Come along, Cattermole come along.

(HARRY *seizes* GIBSON *and throws him round to l.* DOUGLAS *catches* GIBSON, *takes him up L. to c. trying to persuade him to go. Enter* MARSLAND *R. i E. with letter in hand, followed by* CATTERMOLE, *who sits in arm-chair up R.*)

R. CATTERMOLE. DOUGLAS L, GIBSON. MARSLAND. HARRY.

HARRY: Uncle, something very strange has happened; I hope you won't be vexed.

MARSLAND: Well, be quick about it. I've no time to spare.

HARRY: The other day, I made the acquaintance of a gentleman, and he's never seen a meet of hounds, and he's here.

GIBSON: (*who has crossed to* HARRY) Introduce me.

MARSLAND: Well, introduce him.

(GIBSON *is pulling* HARRY'S *coat-tail.* HARRY *knocks his hand away*)

HARRY: (*introducing*) My uncle Marsland Mr. Gibson. (*goes up*)

MARSLAND: How do you do, sir?

GIBSON: How do you do, sir? I'm delighted to make the acquaintance of such a fine old English gentleman! (*surveying him*) Why, bless me, sir, what a noble chest you have! That must be forty-two inches round, (*feeling in pocket for tape*) Where's my. . . (*producing tape*)

(DOUGLAS *pulls at his coat-tail to stop him. then slaps him on the back, and turns up*)

MARSLAND: (*aside*) What an extraordinary man! (*introducing*) Mr. Gib Gib

GIBSON: Gibson, sir.

MARSLAND: Mr. Gibson, Mr. Cattermole. (*goes up to back*)

CATTERMOLE: (*curtly*) How do you do?

(GIBSON *bows extravagantly*)

GIBSON: (*astonished, looking at* DOUGLAS) Cat—Cat

CATTERMOLE: Cattermole. (*spelts*)

GIBSON: How do you do, sir? I'm delighted to make your acquaintance,
    I'm sure, (*looking around at* DOUGLAS) Strange to say I know
    someone named Cattermole. Any relation to (DOUGLAS *who is L.
    up stage runs across quickly, nudges* GIBSON, *then returns to L.*)

DOUGLAS: (*aside to* GIBSON) Shut up!

CATTERMOLE: No. No relation to shut up

(*Enter* JOHN, *R. u. E.*)

JOHN: (*announcing*) Breakfast is ready.

MARSLAND: That's all right! Come along, Cattermole.

HARRY: (*hurrying off R. u. E.*) Come along, Spalding!

(MARSLAND *follows.* DOUGLAS *is hurrying off*)

MARSLAND: (*turning and stopping him*) Certainty not. I've already said
    that Mr. Spalding has his duties to attend to.

(*Exit, R. u. E.* DOUGLAS *turns to go off, L. i E.* GIBSON *tries to speak to
him, but he repels him, and exits.* CATTERMOLE *rises and goes up.* GIBSON
*turns to him, and tries to attract his attention by catching hold of his coat.
Business, and exeunt, R. u. E. Exit* JOHN, *L. u. E. Enter Miss* ASH FORD,
followed by EDITH *and* EVA, *R. i E.*)

MISS ASHFORD: (*coming down to L.*) Now young ladies, our reading.
    You know I promised your father.

EDITH: (*coming c. with* EVA) Oh, I think it's an absurd idea that we
    should work to-day.

EVA: So do I. (*they run up*)

MISS ASHFORD: My dears, you don't call reading work. (*calling off L. i
    E.*) Mr. Spalding, will you kindly prepare the books in the library.

DOUGLAS: (*without*) Certainly.

EDITH: Well, at any rate, we needn't go into that stuffy old library.

EVA: No it's so lovely here.

MISS ASHFORD: Very well, you shall remain here (*calling*)
    Mr. Spalding, will you bring the books here?

DOUGLAS: (*without*) With pleasure.

MISS ASHFORD: Now, young ladies, you see that Mr. Spalding is a
    most accomplished gentleman, so let me again beg of you to keep

up a proper decorum; cease from all fun and nonsense, and behave like young ladies.

EDITH: (*R. demurely*) Yes.

MISS ASHFORD: Yes, you little dove-eyed hypocrite you are the worst of the two. It's you who teach that silly child all her wicked tricks.

EDITH: Well, I will be good, if only for Eva's sake. (*kisses her. EVA waves handkerchief*)

MISS ASHFORD: Be good for your own sake.

EVA: (*at piano wagging handkerchief*) Oh, go on, I don't care.

(*Enter DOUGLAS, L. i E., with heap of books*)

DOUGLAS: Here you are, ladies; I've brought you quite a collection. (EVA *places small table L. of settee; he drops book on it*) The gems of our literature, so they can choose for themselves, eh, Miss Ashford?

MISS ASHFORD: Yes, with the guide, philosopher and friend.

(DOUGLAS *fetches music-stool, and sits behind table,* EVA *places chair L. of table, and sits;* EDITH *sits on settee; Miss* ASHFORD *on chairs, at back,* DOUGLAS *commences to arrange books.* EVA *gets table from behind piano L. and chair from below door L.* EDITH *at once takes a book*—DOUGLAS *puts it back on table then sees* EVA *has taken one, he replaces that and goes up for stool. Both girls retake books and read.* DOUGLAS *comes down with stool sees them takes* EVA's *book, shuts it with a bang.* EVA *jumps. He then takes* EDITH's *she says, "Oh! they were just getting married." He sits looking at her reprovingly.*)

DOUGLAS: First of all (EVA *tries to look over book he has taken up; he withdraws it*) First of all, here's The Vicar of Wakefield.

EVA: I thought so!

EDITH: Oh, we know that by heart.

DOUGLAS: No, by Goldsmith! (*they laugh, he sees the joke*) Well, we'll put the worthy man aside, (*takes up two others*) Mill on Political Economy, Ditto on the Floss, (*they laugh, he puts it aside and takes up another*) Tom Jones by Fielding.

MISS ASHFORD: (*rising and coming down*) Surely that must be a mistake. Tom Jones is a very clever book, but not at all suitable for young ladies, (*girls try to see book*) My dears! my dears!

(DOUGLAS *prevents them, rises and goes to Miss* ASHFORD; *girls talk.*)

DOUGLAS: Have you read it?

MISS ASHFORD: Oh, yes; (DOUGLAS *looks shocked*) that is, no! well a long time ago.

Douglas: Well, I haven't, (*offering, book*) Perhaps you'd like to refresh your memory.

Miss Ashford: (*taking book*) I should like to have the care of the book.

Douglas: (*going back to table and taking another book*) I've got another in your line, Pamela, or Virtue Rewarded.

Miss Ashford: Virtue Rewarded! That must be a very small pamphlet indeed, (*aside going up*) Dear boy, how innocent, he's never read Tom Jones.

(Douglas *sits stool. Girls prepare handkerchiefs*)

Douglas: (*reading*) Milton's Paradise Lost

Miss Ashford: Ah, that's a good book—read that.

Edith: It's awfully dry, but go on, we're listening.

Douglas: Well, Milton was a poet, don't you know.

Eva: No?

Edith: Was he?

Douglas: Well, it says so here; and he was blind, don't you know.

Edith: Poor old chappie!

Douglas: And he dictated Paradise Lost to his daughters, don't you know.

Eva: Poor things!

Douglas: There were only two people in Paradise.

Edith: (*holding up handkerchief tied in a knot*) Adam!

Eva: And Eve! (*business handkerchief, L.*)

Douglas: Quite right! Eve he described as the representative of beauty.

Eva: (*wagging knot*) That's me!

Douglas: Which is nearly allied to evil.

Eva: (*annoyed*) Oh!

Douglas: Adam, on the contrary, was a weak man. (Edith *lets knot drop / all laugh*) In fact, about the weakest man of his time.

(*he examines handkerchiefs amused.*)

Miss Ashford: (*who has come down*) Mr. Spalding! Mr. Spalding! (*they stop laughing and sit straight*) I think you had better read.

Douglas: Better read?

Miss Ashford: Yes, I think the young ladies will understand it better. (*goes back to chair*)

Douglas: All right, (*looks at the girls; all break into a titter;* Edith *whispers in* Douglas's *ear; he laughs;* Eva *says to him "Tell me"; he does so.* DOUGLAS *says "I can tell you a much funnier one than that" puts his arms round their shoulders and whispers. Miss* ASHFORD *says "Oh!" horrified, rises and comes down and looks at them with glasses. They all laugh until* DOUGLAS *looks over his shoulder, and sees Miss* ASHFORD *looking, then all pull up;* DOUGLAS *reads)* "Of man's first" (EVA *tickles his ear with knot)* "Of man's first" (EDITH *same business)* "Of man's first" (*both same business*)

MISS ASHFORD: (*aside*) Now they are fairly started I can go, Poor boy! I wish him joy.

(*Exit, R. u. E.*)

DOUGLAS: (*reading*) "Of man's first"

(EDITH *sees that Miss* ASHFORD *has gone; seizes book from* DOUGLAS *and throws it over his head*)

EDITH: (*running to R.*) She's gone!

EVA: (*rising*) Edith!

EDITH: I couldn't help it, it was so fearfully slow.

DOUGLAS: (*quietly pointing to door*) Do you think she'll come back?

EDITH: No, I don't think she will, (*imitates him*)

DOUGLAS: (*picks up book and gives it to* EVA. *Replacing stool*) Very well, I'm quite at your service. What shall we do? (*up c.*)

EVA: (*replacing table and chair*) We can't play tennis here.

EDITH: No. Let's have some table turning.

DOUGLAS: Oh, table turning's out of date, like planchette. Spiritualism has made such rapid progress.

EDITH: Are you a Spiritualist?

DOUGLAS: Well, no, not exactly. I've had a good deal to do with it lately, though.

EDITH & EVA: (*together*) Really?

DOUGLAS: Yes. (*makes a pass; they start alarmed and run to corners*) Got an uncle who's a medium.

EDITH: Oh, tell us all about it.

(*go to him on R.*)

EVA: Miss Ashford has great thick books about it, but she always hides them from us.

(*go to him on L.*)

DOUGLAS: Well, you must know, then, that the latest thing out is materialization.

EDITH & EVA: (*together*) What's that?

DOUGLAS: They've succeeded in making spirits appear in visible form.

(*repeats pass girls run away as before*)

EVA: Never?

DOUGLAS: (*imitating tone*) Yes! They come bringing violets, and hollyhocks, and cabbages, and buttercups—

EVA: (*eagerly*) And butterscotch butterscotch?

DOUGLAS: Yes. You can shake hands with them.

(*shakes hands with* EVA)

EDITH: (*coming to him*) Really?

DOUGLAS: Yes. And even kiss them.

(*tries to put his arm round* EDITH's *waist and kiss her*)

EDITH: (*running to R.*) Thanks. I'd rather be excused.

EVA: (*close to* DOUGLAS, *meaningly*) Do make a spirit appear. (*she puts her head on his shoulder*)

DOUGLAS: That's not so easy.

EVA: Why not?

DOUGLAS: We require a medium.

EVA: A medium?

EDITH: What's that?

DOUGLAS: A privileged being, whose highly nervous temperament forms a connecting link between the real and spiritual world.

(*mysterious wave of the hands; girls retreat from him frightened*)

EDITH: Do get us a medium, (*returning to him*)

EVA: Yes, please, do.

DOUGLAS: How odd! Miss Ashford has asked me to do the same thing, and I've promised to get her one. But what will your father say?

EDITH: (*excitedly*) Oh, he mustn't know anything about it.

EVA: No. We'll put up the medium at the gardener's. (*runs across to R.*)

DOUGLAS: But Mr. Marsland.

EDITH & EVA: (*together*) Oh! never mind him, etc., etc.

(*Exeunt, R. i E., followed by* DOUGLAS, *remonstrating,* GIBSON *heard without calling, "Yoicks, Yoicks!" Enter* CATTERMOLE, *R. u. E.*)

CATTERMOLE: Confound that fellow! He's perfectly unbearable! The more he drinks the more he talks, the more he talks! the more he drinks.

(*goes to settee and takes up newspaper*)

(*Enter* GIBSON, *intoxicated, R. u. E.*)

GIBSON: Yoicks! Yoicks! Yoicks!

CATTERMOLE: Here, Yoicks, you'll upset your liver if you go on like that.

GIBSON: Yoicks! Yoicks!

CATTERMOLE: You've been taking too much wine, Yoicks. I shouldn't advise you not to take any more, Yoicks.

GIBSON: Oh no. I'm all right. (*coming down*)

CATTERMOLE: Yes, all right and tight!

GIBSON: Jolly thing this hunting breakfast! They're all shouting "Yoicks, yoicks." They've all been to the meet.

CATTERMOLE: Yes, and you've been to the drink.

GIBSON: I wish I hadn't had that champagne. (*walks to settee and pushes against* CATTERMOLE, *making him sit*) Let's sit down and talk.

CATTERMOLE: (*aside*) Confound the fellow! (*aloud, forcing newspaper into* GIBSON's *hand, and taking up another himself*) Here! Go and sit down and read the paper.

GIBSON: I beg your pardon.

CATTERMOLE: You do read the paper sometimes, I suppose.

GIBSON: I hope I didn't hurt you. But you take up so much room.

CATTERMOLE: I say I suppose you can read?

GIBSON: (*going to arm-chair*) Yes, of course, I can read. But I feel too jolly to read now. I'd rather play a game of sst. (*sits*)

CATTERMOLE: I never played it.

GIBSON: A game of whizzt.

CATTERMOLE: You don't know what you're talking about.

GIBSON: I say, I'd rather play a game of whizzt sst.

CATTERMOLE: Whist? I think a little nap would do you more good. Besides, I never play double dummy.

GIBSON: Extraordinary thing! they've taken to printing the paper upside down.

CAITERMOLE: Try it the other way about.

GIBSON: Oh, it's all right now. (*pause*) Oh, I can't see to read. Perhaps it's the lights.

CATTERMOLE: More lkely the liver.

GIBSON: (*dropping paper on knees*) Oh, I can't read.

CATTERMOLE: I thought not! How long do you think the Government will hold out?

GIBSON: (*laughing*) He! he! he! he!

CATTERMOLE: Oh, don't make that "idiotic" noise! I say, how long do you think the Government will hold out?

GIBSON: I was just thinking how long your waistcoat buttons will hold out.

CATTERMOLE: Hem! hem! I was not referring to the corporation, sir. I was speaking of the Government. How long do you think the Government will hold out?

GIBSON: Well, don't fly in a passion. (*rising*)

CATTERMOLE: I don't want to fly. I'm not the figure for flying.

GIBSON: (*crossing to him*) Gentlemen don't quarrel about politics

CATTERMOLE: Gentlemen never quarrel.

GIBSON: No; I'm a gentleman.

CATTERMOLE: Yes, you are!

GIBSON: (*catching hold of* CATTERMOLE's *coat*) Excuse me?

CATTERMOLE Be quiet.

GIBSON: Excuse me

CATTERMOLE: Don't do that!

GIBSON: No but excuse me.

CATTERMOLE: (*rising and crossing to R.*) If you Want a redistribution of seats you can have it.

GIBSON: Excuse me, but your coat's very badly cut.

CATTERMOLE: Who's been cutting my coat?

(*trying to see his back*)

GIBSON: You'll pardon me making the remark but you 'aven't got a fit.

CATTERMOLE: No, but I shall have in a minute if you go on like this.

GIBSON: I'm a judge of these things.

CATTERMOLE: We were not talking of coats we were talking of politics!

GIBSON: Oh, blow politics! (CATTERMOLE *says "I don't want to blow politics."*) Do you know where the fault lies?

CATTERMOLE: Yes, in the Government.

GIBSON: No, in the coat, (*taking hold of him under the arm*) Here, I'll show you in two minutes.

CATTERMOLE: Don't tickle me!

GIBSON: The sleeve's put in all wrong!

CATTERMOLE: Who's been putting my sleeve in wrong?

GIBSON: That coat was made by an ijyot.

CATTERMOLE: It was not, "made in Egypt." It was made in Calcutta.

GIBSON: What cutter?

CATTERMOLE: Calcutta.

GIBSON: I don't know him! Whoever he is, he has made you look an object, (*trying to measure him with newspaper*) Here, I'll measure you for a coat! I'll measure you for a pair of trousers!

(CATTERMOLE *walks round room to L. then R. to avoid Him; he follows.* CATTERMOLE *pushes him on to settee, tearing a piece out of his paper. Enter* DOUGLAS *quickly, R. i E.*)

CATTERMOLE: (*R.*) That fellow's talking like a tailor

DOUGLAS: (*crossing to* GIBSON) I say, Gibson.

GIBSON: That old gentleman's 99 round the waist.

(*on settee back to audience*)

CATTERMOLE: It's a libel!

DOUGLAS: (*going to* CATTERMOLE) Don't take any notice of him. He's an amateur tailor; he's President of the Dress Improvement Society.

(*goes to* GIBSON *who goes L.*)

CATTERMOLE: I'm sorry for the society.

GIBSON: (*with paper to* DOUGLAS) It's all right! I'm reading a leading article.

DOUGLAS: (*to* CATTERMOLE) He had a bad sunstroke. (*c.*)

CATTERMOLE: He ought to be put under restraint

GIBSON: I'll measure him for a sunstroke! Oh, look at his baggy old trousers! I'll measure him for a pair of trousers.

(*Unfolds paper to measure him; it is torn in the shape of a pair of trousers.* CATTERMOLE *points it out to* DOUGLAS, *who rushes at* GIBSON *and forces him off, L. i E., closes door*)

CATTERMOLE: Go and put his head under a pump!

(*Exit, R. u. E.*)

(*Enter* SPALDING, *cautiously, c. from L., with goods and chattels. After looking about, he comes down to settee, sits, and carefully places his goods and chattels on floor in front of him. After placing props in a row neat floats, band-box nearest settee, counts them with finger, finds one short. Counts from other end. Considers. realizes he has goloshes on, removes them and place them end of row. Counts again, satisfied. Places hat on top of settee, smooths hair, handkerchief to nose before he speaks.*)

Thank smodness. here I an? at last!

I've walked over two miles with all my goods and chatels, and I'm half dead! I was obliged to come after that telegram. This seems like city of the dead! I haven't met a soul! They told me in the village that they had all gone to the meet. I suppose there's no harm in my remaining here till someone comes. Oh, dear, I'm so tired! I'll endeavor to take a little repose, (*yawns*)

(*Covers his head with shawl, and lies lack on settee Enter* CATTERMOLE, *R. u. E. with paper*)

CATTERMOLE: (*coming down*) Thank goodness that amateur snip's
  gone! I never met such a vulgar brute in the whole course of my
  life. Now I shall have a chance to read the newspaper in peace.
(*Sits on* SPALDING, *who throws shawl off his head. They turn and recognize
each other. Picture.* CATTERMOLE *rises, putting his foot through band-box.*
SPALDING *tries to pick up the contents.* CATTERMOLE *prevents him. In rising*
SPALDING *throws shawl over* CATTERMOLE'S *shoulders.* CATTERMOLE
*puts orange and bun in his pocket. Draws shawl round him and brandishes
bottle of milk. Picture.* SPALDING *on knees says "You've got my bath bun."*)
CATTERMOLE: How dare you come here, sir? What brought you here?
SPALDING: The train brought me here.
CATTERMOLE: None of your nonsense! What motive?
SPALDING: The locomotive.
CATTERMOLE: Don't you jest with me, sir! I say, what brought you
  here?
SPALDING: D'you know
CATTERMOLE: No, I don't know.
(*strikes hat on settee with bottle*)
SPALDING: Mr. Marsland telegraphed for me to come immediately,
  (*snatching hat away*)
CATTERMOLE: Mr. Marsland acted in perfect good faith; but you've
  no right to come here without my permission.
SPALDING: But I came here to see Mr. Marsland, not you.
CATTERMOLE: (*shouting*) Is Mr. Marsland the principal object or am
  I? Answer me that!
SPALDING: He's beginning again! I shall go back to London and I
  don't like London, (*attempts to run off, c.* CATTERMOLE *catches
  him and drags him back to L.*) Look here, sir, if you will persist in
  behaving in this extraordinary manner, I shall have to be very cross
  with you.
CATTERMOLE: Cross with me! Well, I like that! I shall send you away. I
  shall send you to America. Six months among the Mormons; that'll
  settle you. (SPALDING *says "How nice!"* SPALDING *puts handkerchief to
  his nose; knocking it down*) Don't do that!
(SPALDING *goes to pick it up.* CATTERMOLE *seizes him by the collar; placing
his foot on parcel*)
CATTERMOLE: Here, I must put you in here for the present, (*dragging
  him to L. i E. and looking off*) No, you can't go in there! (*swings him
  round over settee: and takes him up to L. u. E.*) Nor there! (*Ditto to R.*

u. E. and, finally to R. i E., where he slings him off) There! don't you dare come out till I call you! Here's a wreck.

SPALDING: (*putting his head out*) Would you kindly restore to me all my goods and chattels?

CATTERMOLE: (*throwing each article separately. Gags; "There's your goods"* (*bag*), "there's your chattels" (*shawl*), "there's your showerstick" (*umbrella*), "frying-pan" (*hat*), "your Sunday trousers" (*parcel*), "your tobacco pouch" (*golosh*), "portmanteau" (*band-box*)

SPALDING exits and returns says "Pardon me, my periodicals." CATTERMOLE hands "Sunday at Home" showing title saying "There's your War Cry." SPALDING goes, returns, says "My bottle of milk" and runs off,

CATTERMOLE says "Third," throws it. (*It must be caught off. SPALDING returns, says, "Pardon me, my orange." CATTERMOLE says "Play," and bowls it. SPALDING muffs it and CATTERMOLE kicks him off saying "Butter-fingers!"*) And now I must get him away! but how I don't know.

(*Enter Miss* ASHFORD. *R. u. E.*)

MISS ASHFORD: Excuse me, Mr. Cattleshow!

CATTERMOLE: Cattermole! (*spells*)

MISS ASHFORD: Excuse me, Mr. Cattermole, but have you seen a stranger?

CATTERMOLE: No, I have not.

MISS ASHFORD: I thought I saw some one pass in here.

CATTERMOLE: (*angrily*) Well, I've not seen him. Don't you believe me?

MISS ASHFORD: Good gracious! Leave me my nose! (*goes up; exit R. u. E.*)

CATTERMOLE: I don't want your nose. That old fool of a woman's after him now.

(*Enter* DOUGLAS, *L. i E., with* GIBSON's *coat; he is going up stage*)

CATTERMOLE: Hullo! Where are you going with that coat? (*c.*)

DOUGLAS: Oh, I've an uncle who's a pawnbroker.

CATTERMOLE: Another uncle! Brother, I suppose, to the damned good cook. You seem a sensible young fellow so put that coat down and come and talk to me. (DOUGLAS *puts coat on chest*) The fact is, I am in a devil of a fix and I want you to help me out of it.

DOUGLAS: If I can, I will. (*down L. c.*)

CATTERMOLE: Oh you can, because you know this house better than I do. The fact is, I have a nephew.

DOUGLAS: Indeed.

CATTERMOLE: Yes; and he's a blithering idiot.

DOUGLAS: Oh, really.

CATTERMOLE: He's here!

DOUGLAS: (*aside*) By Jove, he's found me out. I thought he would. (*go L.*)

CATTERMOLE: I want you to get rid of him. (*turns up*)

DOUGLAS: I think I can do that.

(*goes L. c. back of settee*)

CATTERMOLE: (*pointing to R. i E.*) I've got him in there!

DOUGLAS: (*surprised, imitating* CATTERMOLE, *pointing*) In there?

CATTERMOLE: Yes, with all his goods and chattels. Now you must get him away. (*goes tip*)

DOUGLAS: But where is he to go?

CATTERMOLE: I don't care, get him away. Take him to London America Kamschatka Potter's Bar Camberwell anywhere.

DOUGLAS: But

CATTERMOLE: Take him to the races and lose him, (*Exit R. u. E. Begin gently lowering lights*)

DOUGLAS: (*coming down to R. i E.*) I wonder who on earth I shall find here? (*opens door, looks in, starts, quickly shuts door, and whistles in astonishment*) Yes, by Jove, you must be got rid of 1 (*calling off*) Mr. Spalding!

SPALDING: Yes.

DOUGLAS: You can come out!

(*goes up and carefully looks off c. and L. u. E.*)

SPALDING: (*going up to him*) Oh! how fortunate to find you here! Has that dreadful man gone?

DOUGLAS: (*running* SPALDING *down to c., looking round cautiously*) Yes, he has gone, but tell me—

SPALDING: Tell you what?

DOUGLAS: How is it you've come here?

SPALDING: Mr. Marsland telegraphed for me to come immediately.

DOUGLAS: Oh, I see, And we had just left?

SPALDING: Yes.

DOUGLAS: But then, how is it that Mr. Cattermole takes you for his nephew?

SPALDING: I haven't an idea! I think the poor old gentleman's a lunatic and he's got my bath bun.

DOUGLAS: Never mind your bath bun, but listen to me.

SPALDING: But I do mind it. I'm so fearfully hungry. D'you know I've had nothing to eat all day and I've such a pain here

DOUGLAS: (*shaking him*) Will you listen to me?

SPALDING: (*resignedly*) Yes. I'm listening.

DOUGLAS: I'm going to take you away, and put you where you where you won't be seen.

SPALDING: Oh, fancy. Very odd! When I was sent for.

DOUGLAS: Yes, I daresay it appears odd, but I haven't time to explain now. So bring your things and come along. (*looks off, L. u. E.*)

SPALDING: (*drops orange*) Oh, I've dropped my orange, (*going up*) I'm sure I've lost half of my goods and chattels.

DOUGLAS: (*returning excitedly and running* SPALDING *down*) Confound it all I too late!

SPALDING: Too late I What's too late? I say, don't frighten me.

DOUGLAS: You can't go out there.

SPALDING: But where am I to go?

DOUGLAS: Oh, I know I I must put you up in the library. (*pushing him towards L. I E.*)

SPALDING: Oh, that'll just suit me.

DOUGLAS: Though there is already some one there.

SPALDING: (*alarmed*) Not that dreadful man?

DOUGLAS: No, though this fellow's a little mad too; but I've no doubt you'll be all right. (*tries to force him through door*)

SPALDING: You'll pardon me, but I 'm getting a little jammed. (DOUGLAS *pushes him off, shuts door, and goes up.* SPALDING *returns; looks carefully about floor.*)

DOUGLAS: (*coming down*) What is it now? What is it now?

SPALDING: I've lost one of my buttons. (DOUGLAS *rushes him off. Putting his head out*) I say, you won't forget, it was a most important button!

DOUGLAS: No! no!

(*throws settee cushion. Hurriedly closes door*)

(*Enter Miss* ASHFORD, *R. u. E.*)

MISS ASHFORD: (*coming down, c.*) Then I did see right. And he is here.

DOUGLAS: (*at door*) Who?

MISS ASHFORD: The stranger I saw enter a little while ago. Who is it?

DOUGLAS: (*aside*) What on earth am I to say?

MISS ASHFORD: Who is it?

DOUGLAS: Miss Ashford you promised to be a motherly friend to me. (*goes c. to her*)

MISS ASHFORD: I did.

DOUGLAS: I claim the fulfilment of that promise now.

MISS ASHFORD: I'm quite ready.

DOUGLAS: (*looking cautiously around*) There is a secret connected with this stranger! He must be hidden for several days.

MISS ASHFORD: (*delighted*) Mr. Spalding! you have gratified the dearest wish of my heart! It is here!

DOUGLAS: What?

MISS ASHFORD: The medium.

DOUGLAS: (*aside*) By Jove, what a good idea.

MISS ASHFORD: Yes; I see it in your face! I asked you to telegraph, and it is here! Now, don't deny it.

DOUGLAS: Well, of course, if you will guess everything, it's no use denying it.

MISS ASHFORD: Oh, this is so good of you; so like your dear mother But now let me see him! (*advancing towards L. I E.*)

DOUGLAS: (*stopping her*) No, no.

MISS ASHFORD: Why?

DOUGLAS: On no account! He's very much exhausted, and must have perfect rest and quiet for tonight.

MISS ASHFORD: These celestial beings are so highly organized. (*points to sky.* DOUGLAS *imitates*)

DOUGLAS: (*pointing to door*) This chap's fearfully highly organized.

MISS ASHFORD: But what shall we do with him? Where shall we put him?

DOUGLAS: I know. We must get him away to the gardener's.

MISS ASHFORD: The very place I Meet me here shortly before dinner. We dine, you know, at eight; it will then be quite dark, and we can get him away unperceived.

(*goes up, gradually lower lights to semi-darkness*)

DOUGLAS: (*follows her*) Very well. I shall expect you.

MISS ASHFORD: I'll go and tell Edith and Eva at once. How can I ever thank you for this great obligation? (*Exit, R. u. E.*)

DOUGLAS: Oh, don't mention it.

(*Enter* HARRY, *L. u. E.*)

HARRY: (*crossing to fireplace*) Well, old fellow, how have you been getting on?

DOUGLAS: I'm half dead! (*sits arm-chair R.*)

HARRY: Anything the matter?

DOUGLAS: Everything's the matter! That fool Gibson got drunk at breakfast. Fortunately, I collared him just as the tailor was coming out; so I've put him away in there! (*pointing to L. i E.*)

HARRY: Then he's all right?

DOUGLAS: But that's not the worst of it! Mr. Spalding, the real private secretary, has turned up.

HARRY: No?

DOUGLAS: He's also in there! (*points*)

HARRY: By Jove, you seem to have quite a collection in there. (*points*)

SPALDING: (*without*) No, I really cannot permit it.

(*off i.. i E.*)

GIBSON: (*without*) What are you talking about, you silly fool? Why don't you talk sense? (*off L. i E.*)

DOUGLAS: (*running to door*) They're actually talking! I should like to have seen the mutual introduction. (*half opens door*)

HARRY: So should I!

SPALDING: (*without*) D'you know—

GIBSON: (*without*) No, I don't know. I can't make head nor tail of what you're saying.

(DOUGLAS *shuts door hastily*)

(*Enter* EDITH *and* EVA, *cautiously, R. i E.; stage dark. From this point to the entrance of* GIBSON, *the characters all speak in half whispers, except* SPALDING, *keeping up the ghostly mysterious line*)

EDITH: (*crosses stealthily*) Mr. Spalding! Are you alone?

EVA: (*crossing stealthily*) Where's the medium?

DOUGLAS: You surely don't really believe—

(HARRY *rattles fire-irons, and runs down; girls scream;* EDITH *falls into* DOUGLAS's *arms,* EVA *into* HARRY's)

(*positions: R.* HARRY, EVA. *and* EDITH, DOUGLAS. *R. all down stage.*)

EDITH: Miss Ashford has told us everything. The gardener's got a room ready, and now we want to see the medium.

EVA: Yes, please; we want to see the medium.

DOUGLAS: But I've already told you that such beings are highly nervous.

HARRY: Yes, please let him have perfect rest and quiet for to-night.

EDITH: What is he like?

EVA: Very creepy, I'm sure.

HARRY: Well, yes, rather.

EDITH: Is he young or old?

DOUGLAS: Well, he's young.

EVA: Young and creepy! How thrilling!

EDITH: Thrilling? I begin to feel quite frightened!

(*Enter* SPALDING, *L. i E.*)

EVA: (*frightened*) But wait until real spirits appear.

SPALDING: (*to* DOUGLAS) Do you know—(*crosses to C.*)

(*Girls scream and run up stage, hide behind curtains.* DOUGLAS *and* HARRY *seize* SPALDING. SPALDING *carried by one hand of each under knee, the other under arm, and throw him off L. I E., struggling and remonstrating. Pause.*)

(*Picture the boys looking at each other in dismay?*)

DOUGLAS: (*crossing to R., to* HARRY) We must get him away to the gardener's.

HARRY: Yes, but we must first get the key. (*c.*)

DOUGLAS: (*going*) Come along then, (*at door R. i E.*)

EDITH: (*running down to* DOUGLAS) Don't go without us!

EVA: (*running down to* HARRY) No, I won't be left here alone.

DOUGLAS: We'll all go together.

HARRY: Yes, we'll all go together!

(*Exeunt, R. i E. Noise without R. i E.* GIBSON *shouting "Don't talk to me." Broken up band-box thrown on after* SPALDING *who has remains of lid round his neck. Enter* SPALDING *greatly alarmed; he closes door and holds It; then runs c.*)

SPALDING: And this is my birthday. Oh, that dreadful man! Why he's worse than the other! He will insist upon measuring me for a strait waistcoat! I little thought that I was coming to be secretary to a private lunatic asylum. I'm not safe!

GIBSON: (*without*) Yoicks! Yoicks! Here, where have you got to go? I'm in the dark! Fetch a candle!

(SPALDING *runs to fireplace*)

SPALDING: (*taking up shovel*) Now, I don't wish to be unkind; but if he attacks me again, I shall give him a good hard knock. (GIBSON *mutters outside*) He seems a little quiet now. Oh, dear! oh, dear! I'm so fearfully tired, and weary, and sleepy, I'll endeavor to take a little repose, (*seats himself in arm-chair*) This is very comfortable! I shall remain here till somebody finds me!

(*Puts handkerchief over head; shovel resting over right arm; moans; and falls asleep*)

(*Enter* DOUGLAS, *R. i E.; looks cautiously around then beckons off to* HARRY.)

DOUGLAS: Come along, Harry!

(*Enter* EDITH, *cautiously; she goes to* DOUGLAS, *followed by* EVA, *with* HARRY.)

EDITH: (*whispering*) Is the coast clear?

DOUGLAS: (*whispering*) Yes. Come along. S-s-sh!

(*They go up stage. They go up in line on tiptoe holding hands turn simultaneously.* SPALDING *moans. All start and turn. Girls cling to* DOUGLAS *and* HARRY.)

EVA: (*seeing* SPALDING) There! there! it's the medium, and it's fast asleep!

(HARRY *advance R, touches* SPALDING, *and pretends to be electrified. All start.*)

HARRY: (*going back to* EVA) All right. I'm here!

EVA: Did it bite?

EDITH: I hope nothing will appear now.

(*Enter Miss* ASHFORD, *R. i E, enveloped in white cloak with hood. All start*)

MISS ASHFORD: Mr. Spalding! Mr. Spalding! (*stumbles against settee*)

DOUGLAS: It's all right it's only Miss Ashford!

EVA: (*to Miss* ASHFORD) Just fancy. The medium's fast asleep.

MISS ASHFORD: Is he? Where? Where?

ALL: (*pointing*) There!

(*mysteriously, simultaneous gesture*)

MISS ASHFORD: So he is!

DOUGLAS: Shall I wake him?

MISS ASHFORD: On no account! It may be a magnetic slumber! See, he embraces a large magnet! The medium may be in ecstasy! (SPALDING *snorts*) He is in ecstasy! Who knows what sublime visions are passing through his mind? (*snore*) It is thus described in the book! First the spirits make themselves heard by knocking! (GIBSON *knocks off*) The knocking is heard! Now, soon the apparitions will glide from the medium.

(*Enter* GIBSON, *enveloped in curtain*)

GIBSON: (*feeling his way*) What infernal nonsense to take away my coat.

MISS ASHFORD: (*waving her hand*) He comes! he comes!

Knocks against GIBSON; screams and falls fainting on settee; when Miss ASHFORD screams, girls do the same; EDITH falls on chair by piano; EVA on chair by fire; SPALDING wakes, rises and strikes GIBSON with shovel. DOUGLAS and HARRY, seeing the state of affairs, arrange in hurried talk what to do; Douglas seizes Gibson and throws him off, L. i *E.*; Harry throws Spalding off, R. i E.; close doors and stand with backs to them as Marsland and Cattermole enter, L. i E., preceded by John with lamp; lights up. Tableau)

Quick Curtain:

Second Picture.

(Spalding *R. i E. and* Gibson *L. i E. threatening each other.* Cattermole *fanning Miss* Ashford *over settee.* Marsland *supporting* Edith *up c. with* Douglas *fanning her.* Harry *on knees fanning* Eva *at fire place.* John *off*)

Curtain.

Act III

SCENE. *Same as Act II. Curtains drawn. Lamp alight on sideboard. Large table with cover in place of small one in Act II., R. Position of chairs at fire-place reversed.* HARRY *discovered seated arm-chair by fire place; reading newspaper*)

HARRY: I wish Douglas would look sharp! He must have been gone nearly twenty minutes, (*rising and looking off; R. i E.*) Spalding is still in there waiting to be taken to a place of safety. (*Enter* DOUGLAS, *L. i E.*) Ah, thank goodness, old fellow, you've come at last! How's Gibson?

DOUGLAS: He's nearly all right now! But how about Spalding?

HARRY: We really must get this fellow out of the house. We've had a very narrow escape! My uncle was, of course, quite convinced that we'd been holding a stance.

DOUGLAS: (*looks off door L. i E.*) But does he know the part that Gibson and Spalding played in it?

HARRY: No, he hasn't an idea; but we really must get him out of the house, (*calling off, R. I E.*) Mr. Spalding!

SPALDING: (*without*) Yes.

HARRY: Will you be good enough to step in here? (*Enter* SPALDING, *R. i E.*) Now, Mr. Spalding, we've got you a room ready, where you will be able to study to your heart's content. But it's not at all necessary that you should appear to-night, you understand?

SPALDING: Perfectly! All I ask for is a little repose and something to eat D'you know, I've had nothing to eat all day, and I have such a pain here. (*drawing his hands across his chest*)

DOUGLAS: I'll ask Miss Ashford to take him some food. (*moves up a little*)

SPALDING: (*crossing to* DOUGLAS) Miss Ashford, did you say? She was my mother's most intimate friend. I shall be charmed to make her acquaintance.

HARRY: Well, so you shall, but ccme along now. (*they are pushing him up to c.*)

SPALDING: (*stopping*) You'll pardon me, but all my goods and chattels are in that room yonder. (*pointing to L. I E.*)

DOUGLAS: I'll fetch them for you. (*Exit, L. I. E.*)

SPALDING: Thanks.

HARRY: Now, Mr. Spalding, you must distinctly understand that you are to remain perfectly quiet,

SPALDING: Oh, yes, from my infancy I've always been accustomed to be seen and not heard.

HARRY: And now you're to be neither seen nor heard. (*c.*)

SPALDING: Very odd! I really don't understand it. (*c.*)

HARRY: I daresay it appears odd, but remember this—if you're discovered you're lost.

SPALDING: Oh, fancy! (*re-enter* DOUGLAS *with goods and chattels which he throws to* SPALDING) Thanks! Thanks! I'm sorry to give you so much trouble.

(DOUGLAS *pushes him up to c. opening*)

HARRY: (*looking off excitedly*) No, no, he can't go out there! Edith's coming up the passage.

DOUGLAS: (*excitedly*) My dear boy, he must!

HARRY: He can't! Quick! quick! (*Theypush him backwards and forwards between them.* SPALDING *says, "Gentlemen, do you take me for a concertina?"*)

(*Pushes* SPALDING *into arm-chair and sits over him with newspaper.* DOUGLAS *stands in front of them. Enter* EDITH, *c.*)

EDITH: Ah, I wanted you! You promised to give me a music lesson, Mr. Spalding. (*crosses to piano L.*)

SPALDING: Oh, I shall be charmed!

DOUGLAS: Charmed! charmed!

(HARRY *puts his hand over* SPALDING's *mouth, then tips up chair*) *throwing him on floor. He then pushes him under table and sits on it.* SPALDING *trips him up. He throws goods and chattels under and sits on end of table*)

EDITH: (*L. c.* DOUGLAS *c. To* DOUGLAS) Why, how odd your voice sounded! Quite far off!

DOUGLAS: Did it? Oh yes! it's a peculiarity of our family. Got an uncle who's a ventriloquist.

EDITH: Really!

DOUGLAS: Yes; such peculiarities often occur in families. You, for instance, I've noticed have a far away expression in your eyes.

EDITH: Have I?

DOUGLAS: Yes, and I've got it in my voice.

(EDITH *goes to piano*)

(*comes down to table. Looks inquiringly at* HARRY *who points under table*)

(*Enter* EVA, *R. U. E.*)

EVA: (*crossing to* EDITH) I'm dying to hear you play, Mr. Spalding.

SPALDING: (*putting his head out at end of table*) Oh, I shall be charmed!

(HARRY *and* DOUGLAS *beat him back girls look;* HARRIS *pretends to be dusting his boots with newspaper*)

EDITH: He's going to give me a music lesson.

DOUGLAS: (*to* HARRY) What on earth am I to do? I don't know a note of music.

HARRY: Oh, you'll be all right! You've only to beat time and count one, two, three, four, you know.

(*goes R. of table*)

EVA: Won't you give us a little music?

(DOUGLAS *goes c.*)

EDITH: Yes, do give us a little music.

HARRY: Yes, do give us a little music, Mr. Spalding. (*amused*)

(DOUGLAS *shakes fist at* HARRY *aside then runs down to beat* SPALDING *back*)

SPALDING: (*putting out head*) I shall be delighted.

(*They beat him back.* SPALDING *puts head out above top end of table and says "D'you know?" They beat him back. Girls looking over music at piano.* HARRY *takes umbrella and sits prepared for hitting his head if it comes out again, but* SPALDING *puts his feet out;* HARRY *puts down umbrella in disgust. Then tells* DOUGLAS *what to say to girls*)

HARRY: (*aside*) Say you've sprained your wrist.

DOUGLAS (*going up to* EDITH) I'm awfully sorry. I should so much have liked to have played you something, but I've sprained my ankle (*catches* HARRY's *eye*) wrist!

EDITH: I'm so sorry!

EVA: What a pity! (*comes down to settee, sits*)

DOUGLAS: (*to* EDITH) But won't you play?

HARRY: Yes, please do.

EDITH: (*taking up a piece of music*) Here's something I think I know. Let's see, it's common time, isn't it?

(DOUGLAS *looks at* HARRY, *he looks at music and nods assent.* HARRY *R. of table.* DOUGLAS *c.*)

DOUGLAS: Y-yes-very!

EVA & EDITH: (*together*) What?

DOUGLAS: Won't you go on? (EDITH *plays.* EVA *on sofa.* HARRY *beats time with news paper rolled up,* DOUGLAS *imitates clumsily. At four he*

looks at HARRY *who nods then tries to stop* DOUGLAS *by waving paper.*
DOUGLAS *not understanding goes faster as* HARRY *waves faster. At*
twenty HARRY *bangs paper on table in despair.* DOUGLAS *goes down*
to table counting, guided by HARRY) One, two, three, four, five, six,
seven, eight, nine, ten, eleven (*to twenty, stopping, to* HARRY) I can't
count any faster. (EDITH *stops playing*)

HARRY: (*after trying to make* DOUGLAS *understand by moving his fingers;*
aside to him) Four, four, four.

DOUGLAS: What for?

EDITH: What a very odd way of counting!

EVA: Yes, very.

DOUGLAS: (*looking at* HARRY) Is it? How do you count?

EDITH: I count one, two, three, four over and over again.

EVA: Of course.

DOUGLAS: (*after a pause, suddenly*) Oh yes, of course! That's the
old-fashioned way mine's the new way. Sometimes I count one
way, sometimes the other; and sometimes I don't count at all! I
say, Harry, you've heard me not count at all. (SPALDING *unseen*
by HARRY *puts feet out.* DOUGLAS *points to the feet then goes up to*
EDITH *at piano*) Won't you go on?

(EDITH *resumes playing.* HARRY *crosses to get to* EVA, *stumbles over*
SPALDING's *feet; he goes back, kicks* SPALDING's *feet and then sits by her*)

HARRY (*taking* EVA's *hand*) Ah, Eva, you would play much better.
Your hands seem made for the piano.

EVA: You are trifling with me.

HARRY: No, don't think that! But let's go out; we can't talk here.

EVA: No, no. I must stay here, or Edith will be cross.

HARRY: No; but listen to me Eva.

(*tries to kiss her*)

EVA: No, no; be quiet I

(EDITH *stops playing.* HARRY *and* EVA *sit apart*)

EDITH: I can't play while they're talking.

DOUGLAS: No; let's stop a littje, till we're undisturbed.

EDITH: You're not a very strict master.

DOUGLAS: I must have some consideration for these delicate little
fingers (*takes hand*)

EDITH: Now, if my cousin Harry were to say that.

DOUGLAS: And may I not also have a heart?

EDITH: I think I had better go on playing.

(*continues playing*)

HARRY: (*to* EVA) Now she's at it again it's all up With talking.

EVA: Well, is it absolutely necessary for us to talk?

HARRY: Yes, Eva darling for I want to tell you that to me you are the dearest little girl upon earth. (*kisses her.* EDITH *strikes chord stops playing; they sit reading again, hidden behind paper*)

DOUGLAS: Now, you know, I really can't give a music lesson like this! (*when* DOUGLAS *speaks* HARRY *and* EVA *start apart, coming down and leaning over settee*) That last passage ought to have been done mezzo-soprano.

HARRY: (*showing him newspaper*) I say, old fellow, here's something in your line! "Wanted, an able-bodied young man to beat the big drum in a travelling circus." (DOUGLAS *returns to* EDITH *with mock dignity*) Oh, I see what it is. We're in the way, we'd better go. (*rises and goes up*)

EVA: (*rising and following* HARRY) Yes, we're in the way, we'd better go!

EDITH: No, stay here, Eva.

EVA: No, we're in the way, we'd better go!

HARRY: (*calls* "DOUGLAS" *twice, he is bending over* EDITH. DOUGLAS *goes to him at c. opening. To* DOUGLAS) "None but a thorough musician need apply." (*Gives* DOUGLAS *paper and exit c. with* EVA; DOUGLAS *throws paper after him*)

EDITH: (*sitting at piano*) And now I can go on playing. (*Plays*)

DOUGLAS: Oh, stop playing and listen to me.

EDITH: (*stopping*) But the music lesson?

DOUGLAS: Every word you utter is music to me. If I could only find a responsive echo in your heart to what I am going to say.

EDITH: (*coming down and sitting on settee*) I don't understand you.

DOUGLAS: (*coming down*) Miss Marsland. Edith, I've only known you for a very very little time, but will you believe me when I tell you that I love you with all my heart? (*over settee*)

EDITH: You have no right to speak to me like this.

DOUGLAS: I know I haven't, but tell me, do you hate the sight of me?

EDITH: No, I don't hate the sight of you.

DOUGLAS: Do you altogether dislike me?

EDITH: No, I don't altogether dislike you.

DOUGLAS: Do you like me a little?

(*holds out hand. She gives hers*)

EDITH: Yes, a little (*he kisses her hand*) a very little.

Douglas: I thought you liked me a little more than a very little; but I see I was mistaken. Will you forgive me?

Edith: (*rising and giving her hands*) Yes, I forgive you. And now, please leave me.

Douglas: Forever?

Edith: No, not so long as that.

Douglas: (*kisses her*) And now to see Mr. Marsland, and make a clean breast of it. (*Exit, L. i E.*)

Edith: What have I done? I ought not to have listened to him, and yet what he said came from the heart. I'm sure he was in earnest! But papa? What will he say? Never mind, I shall tell him nothing, but act for myself. (*Goes up. Spalding moans; she starts and looks about, first at L. u. E., then off c., then comes down L. of table*)

Spalding: Oh! (*crawls out R. from under table*) Why, I must have gone to sleep in my goloshes, (*takes off one golosh keeps it in his hand*) Just fancy my being secretary to a private lunatic asylum, (*seeing Edith*) D'you know (*over R. of table pointing with golosh*)

(Edith *screams and runs round to R. u. E.,* Spalding *following her. Enter* Cattermole, *R. u. E. Picture.* Cattermole *comes between them c. and seizes* Spalding *who has shawl in his hand and now drops it c.*)

Cattermole: (*to* Edith) Don't make a noise, Miss Marsland; you'll alarm the whole house.

Edith: (*crying*) Take him away! the horrid little thing.

Cattermole: (*to* Spalding) There, you hear! the lady says you're a horrid little thing! (Spalding *says, "No she means you!"*) Now then, what are you doing here? (*to* Edith, *who is still crying*) Don't make such a noise! You're making more noise than he is.

Edith: Take it away. Take it away. (*goes down R.*)

Cattermole: My dear, 'it' shall be removed, (*to* Spalding) Now, sir, what are you doing here?

Spalding: Do you know (*points with golosh*)

Cattermole: No, I don't know

(*knocks it out of his hand*)

Spalding: Mr. Marsland (*to* Edith) what have you been saying to this youth?

Edith: I haven't said anything.

Spalding: No, no. Mr. Marsland telegraphed for me to come immediately.

CATTERMOLE: Yes, I know that. You told me that hours ago. Oh, I know what's the matter with you; you've been drinking! (SPALDING *says "No!"* CAT TERMOLE *says*) "Yes you have, you've been with that tailor (*taking him by the coat*) Here, I must put you away again, (*takes him up; drags him to chest*) Here, you must go in here! (*opens chest.* SPALDING *breaks away and comes down L.,* EDITH *alarmed;* CATTERMOLE *comes c.*) Don't be alarmed, Miss Marsland, I'll capture him! (*takes him up and puts him into chest,* SPALDING *is in left corner.* CATTERMOLE *makes mock hypnotic passes at him beckoning him up, he obeys meekly as if fascinated and gets into chest. When he reappears from chest* EDITH *says "Look at him."*) Lie down, and don't make the slightest noise. (*slams lid*)

SPALDING: Would you restore to me all my goods and chattels?

CATTERMOLE: Your goods and chattels, (*gives him wrap*) Here's your wrap if you're not careful you'll get a lot more raps.

SPALDING: How long am I to remain here?

CATTERMOLE: (*banging down lid*) Lie down! (*sits on chest*)

(*Enter Miss* ASHFORD, *R. u.; E., after* SPALDING *knocks in chest*)

MISS ASHFORD: What has happened? Is anything the matter? What's that noise?

CATTERMOLE: That's a Punch and Judy outside.

MISS ASHFORD: Punch and Judy didn't scream.

CATTERMOLE: No, that was Miss Marsland screamed. She's upset her liver, I think. She fancied she saw something somehow somewhat.

MISS ASHFORD: Poor child! I fear the Spiritualism has disagreed with her. Come with me, my dear, and I'll give you something to tranquillize your nerves.

(EDITH *goes to her*)

CATTERMOLE: Yes, that's right. Give her some tranquillizing stuff.

MISS ASHFORD: You want some tranquillizing stuff you wicked old man.

CATTERMOLE: Good evening! Good evening!

MISS ASHFORD: For shame, Mr. Caterpillar!

(*Exeunt Miss* ASHFORD *and* EDITH, *R. u. E.*)

CATTERMOLE: (*opening chest*) Nice trouble you're getting me into! Come up, Jack in-the-Box!

SPALDING: Pardon me. I have a complaint to lodge. (*appears suddenly*)

CATTERMOLE: Where is it?

SPALDING: In the chest.

CATTERMOLE: That's your liver!

SPALDING: No; the ventilation of this chest is most Inefficient.

CATTERMOLE: Can't help that. I'm not a Sanitary Inspector.

SPALDING: I'm so fearfully hungry! I've had nothing to eat all day, and have such a pain here.

CATTERMOLE: You're a perfect cormorant, you are. (*giving him golosh*) Here's your golosh, eat that! And now lie down! And remember if you are discovered you are lost!

SPALDING: Pardon me, if I am discovered I am found.

CATTERMOLE: Lost!

SPALDING: Found!

CATTERMOLE: Lost! (*bangs lid down*)

SPALDING: (*opening lid*) Found!!

CATTERMOLE: Lost!!! (*bangs lid down*)

SPALDING: (*popping up*) D'you know, I've taken quite a dislike to you.

CATTERMOLE: (*banging down lid*) And now to find the secretary to get him away. (*Exit, L. u. E.*)

(*Enter Miss* ASHFORD, *R. u. E.*)

MISS ASHFORD: Edith has told me the cause of her fright. Poor child, to be left alone with a medium! Oh, that I had been in her place! What chances what some people have only to throw them away. But stay! He may still be hovering about! Perhaps the magnetic influence which Dr. Bogus tells me I possess may serve to call him back. I'll try! I'll try! (*waves arms in the air, looking upwards.* SPALDING *thumps in chest. Miss* ASHFORD *walks down to R. corner*) He hears! He raps and I am rapt!

SPALDING: (*opening chest, and rising*) It is impossible for me to remain here any longer, (*sees Miss* ASHFORD) This is evidently one of the female patients. The poor soul imagines she is swimming! I'll speak to her. (*to her*) Dear lady!

MISS ASHFORD: (*seeing him*) Ah! 'tis he! 'tis he! and my fondest hope is realized.

SPALDING: I beg your pardon.

MISS ASHFORD: Nay, never beg my pardon! What an honor! What an honor!

SPALDING: (*aside*) The poor soul's very mad! I'll hold converse with her. (*getting out of chest*)

MISS ASHFORD: He comes! He comes by instalments!

SPALDING: (*coming down to her t R.*) Dear lady I implore you—

MISS ASHFORD: Nay, never implore me! Rather let me implore you. Let us hold converse together. Let us journey together. Let us fly together.

SPALDING: Where?

MISS ASHFORD: Into the realms of the spirit world!

SPALDING: But may I not first tell you my story?

MISS ASHFORD: Would that I had time to hear it (*leading him to settee*) for it must be an interesting one, but time presses; might we not employ the moments better? (*sits on settee*)

SPALDING: This is most embarrassing! She is evidently an amorous lunatic! I hope she won't make love to me (*turns L. to go up, she putts him down by his coat-tail he sits L. of her*)

MISS ASHFORD: Ah, do not leave me! The risk we run of being discovered is enormous, the danger great, yet would I dare all for is not the opportunity priceless?

SPALDING: Quite so quite so. But why should we mind being discovered, dear lady?

MISS ASHFORD: Brave creature! You care nought for bodily ills. But know this if you are discovered you are lost!

SPALDING: (*aside*) That is evidently a password of some kind.

MISS ASHFORD: But why waste the time in idle talk? Teach me, oh teach me! You'll find me an attentive pupil. See, here I will sit at your feet. Let me learn something of the secrets of your mystic calling.

SPALDING: (*rising*) She's evidently a lunatic of the most advanced type. Would I had remained in the chest. (*goes up to chest*)

MISS ASHFORD: (*going, R.*) He doesn't answer. His mind is absent! Time presses and I must recall him to the present. (SPALDING *has got quickly into chest and closed lid. Miss* ASHFORD *turns, gives a little scream and says "Gone!" He reappears slowly raising lid with head then gets out and stands meekly in front of chest. Aloud*) Ah, do not leave me, I pray you, gentle spirit, do not vanish. Who would dream what power, what intellect, what massive strength lies hidden behind that gentle exterior.

SPALDING: Quite so, quite so.

MISS ASHFORD: But for the secrets of your mystic calling if you knew how I hunger!

SPALDING: (*who has come down*) Dear lady, so do I.

MISS ASHFORD: But you can always attain your wishes.

SPALDING: I wish I could.

MISS ASHFORD: Then you do acknowledge a superior in your calling?

SPALDING: Be seated, dear lady! once more. (*leads her to settee. they sit*)

MISS ASHFORD: Ah.

SPALDING: Quite so. Dear lady, I'm going to ask you a favor.

MISS ASHFORD: Ask me a favor?

SPALDING: Yes. Will you grant it?

MISS ASHFORD: Whatever lies in my poor power.

SPALDING: Can you get me a ham sandwich?

MISS ASHFORD: A ham sandwich?

SPALDING: Yes, or a bath bun.

MISS ASHFORD: A bath bun?

SPALDING: D'you know I've had nothing to eat all day, and I have such a pain here.

MISS ASHFORD: Poor martyr! Yes, this poor shell must be supplied; it won't take much, (*rising*) But you must remain concealed till I can take you to a place of safety. (*taking him up*)

SPALDING: You're not going to hide me, are you?

MISS ASHFORD: Only for a few moments.

SPALDING: D'you know, I've been hiding all the mnorning. I never had such a hiding before!

MISS ASHFORD: (*taking him to chest*) Here!

SPALDING: Pardon me, not in the chest. Think of the Mistletoe. Bough.

MISS ASHFORD: (*drawing curtains*) Behind these curtains, you may remain concealed.

SPALDING: But the draught.

MISS ASHFORD: I will bring you one immediately.

SPALDING: D'you know, I've had nothing to quench my thirst all day but an acidulated drop.

MISS ASHFORD: Poor martyr! but remain there, and I will return immediately with viands of the choicest.

SPALDING: I should prefer the ham sandwich.

MISS ASHFORD: You shall have it, but remember this if you're discovered, you're lost. (*Exit R. u. E.*)

SPALDING: It is a password. (*draws curtain*)

(*Enter* CATTERMOLE, *L. u. E.; goes to chest. Enter* HARRY, *R. u. E., looks under table*)

CATTERMOLE: Now, to get this miserable worm (*Opens chest astonished*) Why, the worm's gone!

(*slams down lid. At once* HARRY *turns; jumps sitting on table.* CATTERMOLE *sits simultaneously on chest*)

HARRY: (*alarmed looks round*) Ah, how do you do?

CATTERMOLE: (*imitating*) How do you do?

HARRY: I'm looking for something I've mislaid.

CATTERMOLE: I've mislaid something I'm looking for. (*peeps into vase on piano*)

(*Enter* GIBSON, *L. I E.*)

GIBSON: (*looking off*) Here, none of your cheek!

CATTERMOLE: Oh, here's that tailor fellow. I cant Stand him. (*Exit, L. u. E*)

JOHN: (*without*) Ah, yes, you're all right now, sir.

GIBSON: (*to* HARRY) I say, that flunkey's deuced impertinent.

HARRY: Never mind the flunkey, Mr. Gibson, but listen to me. In consequence of your behavior this morning, my uncle has ordered your things to be taken to the station.

GIBSON: Oh, don't say that! I'll apologize. A gentleman can apologize.

HARRY: Yes, but not in your case. I'm sure you can blame no one for this but yourself,

GIBSON: You don't mean to say that I'm to go?

HARRY: I do! Exactly! (*Exit, R. i E.*)

GIBSON: Confound it, this is a nuisance! Just as I was getting on so well, too. Well I suppose it's only the gentlemanly thing to do; so I'll be off. I shall be able to call again and apologize, and perhaps get on visiting terms, (*going up;* SPALDING *puts his feet behind curtains; he sees them*) Why, that's a couple of feet! (*retreating*) There's a man concealed behind that curtain. Perhaps it's a burglar! If it is, here's my chance of distinguishing myself. I'll get into their good graces, (*taking up shovel and tongs*) I'll attack him! I'll show them I can be a man if they don't think I'm a gentleman, (*advancing, frightened, to curtains.* SPALDING *rests one foot on top of the other*) No, by the look of the feet he must be a brawny ruffian! On second thoughts I'll ring for assistance, (*rings bell*) that's the safest plan. I shall be the means of punishing the scoundrel and earning Mr. Marsland's eternal gratitude, (*enter* JOHN, *L. i E. banging him with shovel*) Here, there's a man concealed behind those curtains! (JOHN *makes for door, L. i E.;* GIBSON *pulls him back with tongs*) Don't run away. Run for assistance, and bring a stout cord to bind him with. You understand?

JOHN: Yes, sir. (*Exit, L. i E.*)

GIBSON: I shall be able to curry favor with Mr, Marsland, expose that infernal young Cattermole without hurting myself, and stand upon my dignity as a gentleman if they'll only give me a chance!

(*Re-enter* JOHN *with cord*)

GIBSON: Don't be frightened! (GIBSON *R. and* JOHN *L. points to curtains encouraging each other to go first. They go up on tiptoe together.* SPALDING *drops one foot off the other. They start back. Repeat bus. and advance and draw curtains right back simultaneously*) Seize him, bind him and I-I-I'll find Mr. Marsland. (*Exit hurriedly, R. u. E.*)

(*disclosing* SPALDING *sitting, reading "Sunday at Home" he looks up quietly*)

JOHN: Now, then, what are you doing here?

SPALDING: I'm reading the Sunday at Home.

JOHN: Come along!

(*seizes him, pushes him roughly into chair, c., and binds him to it*)

SPALDING: (*aside*) This is evidently one of the yarders. Now for the password! (*aloud*) If you are discovered you are lost.

JOHN: Yes, and sent to the lock-up.

SPALDING: Would you kindly explain to me the meaning of this treatment?

JOHN: You'd better be very careful what you say. It will all be taken down as evidence against you. (*retires to back*)

(*Enter* CATTERMOLE *and* MARSLAND, *L. u. E.*)

CATTERMOLE: The worm! (*goes down L.*)

MARSLAND: What's all this about?

SPALDING: That's just what I've been asking this gentleman.

MARSLAND: But what are you doing here?

SPALDING: Well, by this time I really don't know.

JOHN: Oh, sir, he's a desperate character! We found him hiding behind the curtains.

MARSLAND: Well, have you tied him up?

JOHN: Yes, sir.

MARSLAND: Then you may go! (*exit* JOHN, *c.*)

(*Enter Miss* ASH FORD, *with basket, R. i E.*)

MISS ASHFORD: (*at table*) What! Is it possible? Oh, joy! What a triumph! Is he going to do it? Is he going to show you how it's done; Now, Mr. Marsland, you will believe me, won't you? He can't have any accomplices here!

MARSLAND: (*crossing to her*) But what have you got there?

MISS ASHFORD: Something for him. Poor fellow, he's had nothing to eat all day.

MARSLAND: For him! (*points to* CATTERMOLE *who growls dissent*) For whom?

MISS ASHFORD: The medium.

MARSLAND: A medium in my, house! Where is he?

MISS ASHFORD: There, before your eyes.

(CATTERMOLE *looks pityingly at Miss* ASHFORD, *pointing to head and shaking head*)

CATTERMOLE: That thing a medium! Well, he doesn't look a very happy medium! But there, I disown him, I cast him off! I'll have nothing more to do with him.

SPALDING: Well, there's some comfort in that! Will some one release me from this invidious position? Would you kindly untie me?

MARSLAND: Oh, untie

MISS ASHFORD: (*interrupting*) No, you must do that yourself, and then you'll float around the room, won't you? And you'll make him float, won't you? (*to* CATTERMOLE)

CATTERMOLE: No, no, you won't! You'd upset my liver!

MARSLAND: Miss Ashford, your Spiritualism is turning your brain.

(*Enter* KNOX *c. from L.*)

MARSLAND: What do you want?

KNOX: Beg pardon, sir, the servant told me I should find Mr. Cattermole here.

CATTERMOLE: Well, here I am! What on earth do you want with me?

KNOX: No, sir. Not you! Mr. Cattermole, junior. Mr. Douglas Cattermole. (*sees* SPALDING) Ah, here he is! I serve you with that writ! (*sticks it in his collar; going*)

SPALDING: If you are discovered you are lost.

MARSLAND: Stop a moment, my good man! How do you know that this is Mr. Douglas Cattermole?

KNOX: Why, sir, from the description. "Believed to be at Mr. Marsland's, disguised in clerical attire". (*Exit, c. to L.*)

MARSLAND: Mr. Cattermole, I appeal to you. Is this young man your nephew?

CATTERMOLE: That thing? Yes, I'm sorry to say he is. (*goes up L.*)

(*Enter* GIBSON, *R. u. E.*)

GIBSON: Ah, Mr. Marsland, how glad I am to find you here. Sir, I've saved you no inconsiderable loss. I don't know what would have 'appened if I had not been here.

MARSLAND: Much obliged to you for your good intentions, Mr. Gibson.

MISS ASHFORD: Mr. Spalding knew of his arrival. Perhaps Mr. Spalding can explain.

SPALDING: What's the use of explaining, dear lady? No one will listen.

MISS ASHFORD: Oh, but Mr. Spalding has great weight in this household.

SPALDING: Well, I should never have thought it.

(*Enter* DOUGLAS, *L. i E.*)

DOUGLAS: (*aside*) By Jove! they've unearthed the parson! (*L. corner*)

SPALDING: (*rising and coming down, c.*) Ah! (SPALDING *being tied to chair brings it with him. As he rises legs of chair hit* GIBSON's *shins who is crossing at back to* CATTERMOLE) here's my friend! Would you kindly—

DOUGLAS: (*aside to him*) Say you're Cattermole.

SPALDING: Say my Catechism? (DOUGLAS *goes L.*)

MARSLAND: (*to* DOUGLAS) This person in the chair here appeals to you. There's some mystery about all this. Will you be good enough to explain?

(*Enter* EDITH, *R. u. E., followed by* EVA *and* HARRY. EDITH *comes down R. C. on* MARSLAND's *L.* EVA *and* HARRY *go to fireplace.* SPALDING *with chain, C. looking round helplessly.* GIBSON *comes down on* DOUGLAS *R.* CATTERMOLE *comes to back of settee*)

EDITH: Papa dear, the dinner-bell has rung such a long time.

MARSLAND: But there's some mystery.

GIBSON: (*to* DOUGLAS) So you've got the writ, eh, Mr. Spalding?

SPALDING: Yes, this is the second time I've had it.

GIBSON: You! (*taking writ from his collar*) Did Knox give it you? I don't want you, my good man. (*pushes him away; he falls on settee; to* DOUGLAS, *giving him writ*) I serve you with this writ, Mr. Douglas Cattermole.

ALL: Douglas Cattermole!

CATTERMOLE: That's Mr. Spalding, Mr. Marsland's private secretary.

GIBSON: I beg your pardon, sir, that is Mr. Douglas Cattermole, who owes me, Sydney Gibson, of Bond street 300 pounds. (*L. of settee*)

CATTERMOLE: (*imitating*) Very well, Mr. Sydney Gibson of Bond-street, you shall have your 300 pounds. (*to* DOUGLAS) So, then you are my nephew!

DOUGLAS: Yes. (*goes to him.* GIBSON *goes L.*)

CATTERMOLE: Then what do you mean by masquerading at my friend's house in this manner?

DOUGLAS: I've been trying to sow my wild oats.

CATTERMOLE: And so you drink something stronger than tea?

DOUGLAS: Yes.

CATTERMOLE: And do you read the Pink 'un and the Blue 'un and the Winning Post?

DOUGLAS: Yes.

CATTERMOLE: And you make a book on the races?

DOUGLAS: Yes sometimes.

CATTERMOLE: Come to my arms, then, you're my nephew after all.

(*they embrace.* EDITH *goes up to c. opening.* DOUGLAS *joins her*)

MARSLAND: (*to* SPALDING) Now, sir, if you're not Mr. Douglas Cattermole who the devil are you, and what are you doing in my house?

SPALDING: D'you know

ALL: No!

SPALDING: Mr. Marsland telegraphed for me to come immediately.

MARSLAND: I telegraphed for you?

SPALDING: Yes. I came here to be secretary to your private lunatic asylum.

MARSLAND: My private lunatic—

GIBSON: (*to* SPALDING) Oh, so you're not a burglar?

SPALDING: No.

MISS ASHFORD: And you're not a medium?

SPALDING: No.

CATTERMOLE: And you're not my nephew?

SPALDING & CATTERMOLE: (*together*) No, thank goodness, not.

MARSLAND: Then your name is—

SPALDING: Robert Spalding.

MISS ASHFORD: Robert Spalding! (*crossing to him*) Then you are my dear little Bobby kins after all? (*kisses him*)

ALL: Miss Ashford!

MISS ASHFORD: I was his mother's dearest friend, and I will be his friend.

(*They go up, behind settee.* GIBSON *unties chair and she gives him sandwiches from basket*)

CATTERMOLE: (*to* MARSLAND) Our old scheme can now be carried out. My nephew's a fine presentable young fellow, and can marry your daughter; and from what I can see, they've already settled it between them.

DOUGLAS: (*coming down with* EDITH *c.*) Yes, Mr. Marsland, Edith has consented subject to your approval to become my wife.

EDITH: Yes, please, papa, we want to get married.

MARSLAND: Married! Rubbish! Just look at Eva; she's far more sensible.

HARRY: (*down R. with* EVA) Yes, uncle, she's sensible enough to take me.

CATTERMOLE: Come! Come! You can't have any objection. You know you're pleased as Punch. I say, do you remember the last wedding we went to you had a drop too much of the—(*all laugh*)

MARSLAND: (*trying to silence him*) Hush! Well, I suppose I must give way! (*to* DOUGLAS) Here, take her!

DOUGLAS: Thank you, sir. Exchange, they say, is no robbery and though I have taken from you your daughter, I've found you what you long needed.

CURTAIN.

A Note About the Author

Charles Hawtrey (1858–1923) was an English actor, director, producer, manager, and playwright. Specializing in comedy, Hawtrey earned a reputation as a leading performer of the Victorian era whose work and mentorship inspired such figures as Oscar Wilde, Somerset Maugham, and Noël Coward. After struggling to establish himself as an artist, he launched his career with *The Private Secretary*, an adaptation of a popular German farce involving the relationship between a clergyman and two irreverent, indebted young men. Knighted for his work in theater, Hawtrey starred in several silent movies toward the end of his life, making him a vital resource for tradition and expertise in a time when the dramatic arts saw extensive stylistic and technological change. Knighted in 1922, Hawtrey was a monumental figure in English theater who adapted with the times he served to define.

A Note from the Publisher

Spanning many genres, from non-fiction essays to literature classics to children's books and lyric poetry, Mint Edition books showcase the master works of our time in a modern new package. The text is freshly typeset, is clean and easy to read, and features a new note about the author in each volume. Many books also include exclusive new introductory material. Every book boasts a striking new cover, which makes it as appropriate for collecting as it is for gift giving. Mint Edition books are only printed when a reader orders them, so natural resources are not wasted. We're proud that our books are never manufactured in excess and exist only in the exact quantity they need to be read and enjoyed.

bookfinity™

Discover more of your favorite classics with Bookfinity™.

- Track your reading with custom book lists.
- Get great book recommendations for your personalized Reader Type.
- Add reviews for your favorite books.
- AND MUCH MORE!

Visit **bookfinity.com** and take the fun Reader Type quiz to get started.

Enjoy our classic and modern companion pairings!

Classic & Modern